The Dancers'
Body Book

also by Allegra Kent
Allegra Kent's Water Beauty Book

The Dancers'
Body Book

ALLEGRA KENT

with

James and Constance
Camner

William Morrow and Company, Inc.
New York 1984

Copyright © 1984 by Allegra Kent, James Camner and Constance Camner

Grateful acknowledgment is extended to James J. Camner, Steven Caras, Hank O'Neil, W. J. Reilly, and Martha Swope, for permission to reproduce photographs.

Library of Congress Cataloging in Publication Data

Kent, Allegra.
  The dancers' body book.

  1. Physical fitness.   2. Dancers—Attitudes.
3. Nutrition.   4. Exercise. I. Camner, James.
II. Camner, Constance.   III. Title.
GV481.K43   1984   613.7'1   83-17360
ISBN 0-688-02211-1
ISBN 0-688-01539-5 (pbk.)

Printed in the United States of America

First Edition

1 2 3 4 5 6 7 8 9 10

BOOK DESIGN BY MARIA EPES

FOREWORD

Just about everyone is dieting these days, but dancers are more successful at it than most other people.

Of course, the daily classes and rehearsals of a ballet company help dancers burn off calories and keep their figures trim. Yet, as the dancers themselves will explain, they need to be thinner than the rest of the general public and still eat enough to maintain energy and stamina levels. How do they do it?

This book will answer that question, and many others as well, about how dancers build and maintain some of the most beautiful bodies in the world—and about how you, the reader, can take advantage of their experiences with diet, health and exercise.

Dancers have a special attitude toward their bodies. It comes from their constant critical attention to their technique, form and appearance.

As the public has become more conscious of losing weight and improving health, dancers too have become thinner and stronger through the influence of choreographers and stars. More than just a popular trend or a fashion fad, however, the slenderness of ballet dancers is a way of life. As Marika Molnar, physical therapist for the New York City Ballet, observes, "Ballet keeps up with society. It is moving fast and the choreography is fast—fast and hard. In order to keep up with that, dancers have to make adjustments to help their bodies as well."

In the following chapters you'll discover how dancers make

Allegra Kent with Anthony Blum in *Dumbarton Oaks*, choreographed by Jerome Robbins. (*Photo copyright © 1983 by Martha Swope*)

those adjustments—their diets, their special tips, their favorite exercises, even their own recipes. The dancers' secrets to being thinner, healthier and having more energy will be revealed, not only for aspiring dancers to enjoy and take advantage of, but for the general public to learn from and emulate.

Through a great many revealing personal interviews with dancers, from the youngest soloists to the most famous superstars of ballet, you'll be finding out a lot about them that you might never have expected.

And you'll be learning about the ways that you too can apply what works for dancers to your own, non-dancing lifestyle.

ACKNOWLEDGMENTS

I want to thank my colleagues in the ballet world who, by sharing their thoughts on diet and fitness, made this book possible. Along with the dancers were the many friends who also contributed their time and kind efforts to *The Dancers' Body Book*.

Merrill Ashley; Mikhail Baryshnikov; Toni Bentley; Jean-Pierre Bonnefous; Isabel Brown; Fernando Bujones; Dierdre Carberry; Christopher D'Amboise; Jacques D'Amboise; Alexandra Danilova; Parmenia Migel Ekstrom; Suzanne Farrell; Peter Fonseca; Alexander Goudenov; Cynthia Harvey; Susan Jaffe; Mary Kasakove; Darci Kistler; Tobias Leibovitz; Natalia Makarova; Patricia McBride; Marika Molnar; Doris Pearlman; Muriel Stuart; Mel Tomlinson; Martine van Hamel; Edward Villella; Heather Watts; Nancy Zeckendorf.

CONTENTS

Foreword   7

Acknowledgments   11

CHAPTER ONE: *Why Dancers Need to Diet— You Can't Fool Anyone When You're Wearing Tights*   17

CHAPTER TWO: *The Dancers' Secret*   37

CHAPTER THREE: *The Dancers' Diet*   53

CHAPTER FOUR: *A Diet to Live By*   75

CHAPTER FIVE: *Food for Dance: Dancers' Recipes —Low-Calorie and Otherwise*   103

CHAPTER SIX: *The Chain Around the Refrigerator*   125

CHAPTER SEVEN: *Ballet, the Oldest Beauty Exercise*   133

CHAPTER EIGHT: *Dancers' Serious Exercise*   151

· Contents

CHAPTER NINE: *Fun and Games*   165

CHAPTER TEN: *A Healthy Outlook*   183

CHAPTER ELEVEN: *Seven Diet Sins*   203

APPENDIX: *The Reading List*   219

The Dancers'
Body Book

CHAPTER ONE

Why Dancers Need to Diet—You Can't Fool Anyone When You're Wearing Tights

The number-one reason dancers have to diet is the merciless exposure of their bodies in class and onstage. Even certain costumes can work against them, making them appear heavier or revealing an unattractive feature, and that's especially true of tights.

You can't fool anyone when you're wearing tights. Ounces become pounds under a leotard. Any extra weight is as easily noticed by the people in the back row as it is by the people in the front.

No question about it, a leotard is probably more revealing than nudity. A dancer can look pretty terrible in tights unless she's pared her weight down to the absolute minimum. There's no in-between.

That's why I worry less about my weight when I'm dancing the roles that call for nightgowns as costumes instead of tights. There is nothing like an upcoming performance in a leotard to put the fear of fat into you!

If a dancer really needs a reason to diet, tights will do it every time. Peter Fonseca, a dancer with American Ballet Theatre, says, "Suddenly I'm feeling ten pounds overweight and there's a performance coming up and they say, 'You have to wear white

Peter Fonseca of ABT in *Les Rendezvous* by Frederick Ashton. *(Photo copyright © 1983 by Martha Swope)*

tights.' You have to be skinny and you have to appear even skinnier, or you're going to look fat onstage.

"The management tells you this, you know. They'll say, 'You have to lose weight.' Even though I've already been trying to lose and maybe have lost about five pounds, getting down to the low hundred-forties, I'll just have to get down to rock bottom, which for me is about one hundred thirty-two."

It's pretty tough for the poor dancer who works hard to stay slim and look good, and *still* feels fat in a white leotard.

But it isn't just the fear of tights that makes dancers try to be as thin as possible. The pressure to stay slim comes from everywhere: the audience, the management, even fellow dancers. In the New York City Ballet that encouragement came from George Balanchine and the teachers, but always as an unspoken wish. Dancers often know without being told that staying slim is what is required of them.

Isabel Brown, who danced with ABT in the 1940's and whose daughter Leslie, star of *The Turning Point*, is with the company today, talks about the differences in appearances. "When I was in the American Ballet Theatre, most of the dancers were really quite chunky, and in those days it was considered okay not to be skinny-skinny. But about ten years after I left American Ballet Theatre it was actually Balanchine who started with 'the stick' —you know, the very thin dancers."

Often the look of the modern ballerina is attributed to the influence of Balanchine. "In the early days, you know, everyone thought Mr. Balanchine wanted a string bean with a leg all the way up to here. . . ." says Muriel Stuart, pointing somewhere near her shoulder to show what she means. As the last protégée of the legendary Anna Pavlova and an instructor at the School of American Ballet, Muriel is in a unique position to observe the comings and goings of ballet fads. "Well, of course, that wasn't even partly true. After all, he had to use the material that was at hand. But he wanted a body that was supple—a long, thin body. It can be the most beautiful."

Isabel Brown agrees. "That look still prevails today, and it's really a wonderful look, if they aren't too, too thin. I think that a heavy dancer onstage—not even heavy, but a normal 'heavy' —takes away from the illusion of beauty that you expect from a dancer with great grace.

"Particularly with females, you expect them to look superior. A man might carry a normal weight. Because they're men, they don't have to be too thin."

(Unless of course they're wearing white tights!)

A new principal dancer with ABT, Cynthia Harvey, says, "Even though it's easier to know I'll be in a romantic tutu instead of a leotard, it really doesn't change the pressure much, because the line always looks better when it is long and thin."

But some dancers have an easier time of it than others. People with certain body types, those that naturally possess a long and slender line, can be casual about watching what they eat and still keep the right look, while the rest must constantly work to lower their weight and get rid of the fat that seems to cling to those terrible problem areas.

It isn't always just a matter of weight, either. A short, chunky girl, for example, might weigh less than a tall, thin girl. But the poor short dancer will have to diet twice as hard as the tall one to get a ballerina's ethereal look.

Cynthia tries to take that fact into account when she is dieting. "Even though I'm thin-boned, it doesn't always spread evenly when it comes."

Like most other dancers, Cynthia is practical and frank about her weight. She is conscious of any extra pounds and sets her own weight-loss goals accordingly.

"I still want to lose five pounds," she says. "My ideal weight would be ninety-nine to a hunded one pounds. I'm five feet four and a quarter inches—I look taller, but am not all that tall— and I usually have a working weight of a hundred six pounds. I feel strong at a hundred six.

"My partners might be more appreciative if I were thinner—

even the strongest of them. Baryshnikov lets me know without saying anything. He'll groan a little, or he'll grab at the area in question. That lets you know! And if you're going to be dancing with him, you certainly want to make yourself look good."

On the whole, however, male dancers are understanding about a ballerina's struggle to stay thin. As much as they might like to lift feathers or support a twig through a pirouette, they don't want their partners to hurt themselves, and they certainly want them to look as good as possible.

One of today's most spectacular male dancers is American Ballet Theatre star Fernando Bujones, who says, "Of course we prefer lighter ballerinas, but we also like to see beautiful ballerinas, and not all bones, either for female or male."

Fernando's own weight problem, however, is a tendency to *lose* too much weight if he's not careful. "I'm lucky. I wind up losing about five or six pounds after a major season at the Met in New York."

His concern, naturally, is not so much with his appearance as it is with his health. This attitude is not Fernando's alone, however.

Every professional dancer must pay critical attention to his or her health needs. Diet and proper nutrition are high on that list, and not only for beautiful bodies, but for strong, healthy bodies onstage and off. All dancers need to be careful to maintain trim figures on the one hand, but not to drop below the level where losing pounds might mean losing strength or stamina on the other. Fernando is fortunate in that he has a happy and close family to see that he eats exactly what he needs for his demanding career.

As you can see, this concern about diet is a real and very serious thing for dancers. Sometimes those extra pounds can mean the difference between what roles they get, or what partners want to dance with them, or even in getting a job in the first place.

"Before I joined the company, I weighed a hundred ten

Susan Jaffe of ABT stretching backstage at the Metropolitan Opera House in New York. (*Photo copyright © 1983 by James J. Camner*)

pounds and I was heavy," says young Susan Jaffe, who is now making a very fine name for herself with American Ballet Theatre. "The staff told me I had to lose weight before I could join the company."

Susan went to great lengths to lose the weight—what young dancer wouldn't with a chance to join a major company? "I went to a diet doctor. It was very slow. I also found that I was getting really tired.

"But what was good about it was that I learned which foods really put on weight. Unless you have a weight problem, you don't know how many calories you're putting into your mouth when you pick up food. You just don't think about it. I know I never used to think about how many calories there were in the mayonnaise or in my tuna-fish salad. You just don't say, 'Oh, my gosh, seventy extra calories!'

"The diet worked, but I couldn't stick to it. Finally, I just fasted. I drank a lot of iced tea, because it was during the summer. Somehow, by drinking a lot of liquids I kept myself going. But after I lost the weight I wanted to lose, I actually had to reteach myself how to eat."

It might seem unthinkable to the average person that at 110 pounds Susan weighed too much. Even though she's 5'5" and can carry 110 pounds quite easily, she wasn't a *thin* dancer. Now she weighs an attractive 102 pounds, a weight she feels is "normal."

It might seem as though a lot of the dancers' thin look is just a matter of fashion—and one that has changed significantly over the past thirty years and more. Madame Alexandra Danilova, the legendary ballerina of Ballets Russes fame and now a revered teacher at the School of American Ballet, agrees that today's obsession with weight is an American trend. "In Russia, nobody told you, 'You must get thinner.' I wouldn't say the dancers were slender, but they were not fat—just normal.

"But in the West, seeing ballet dancers in their leotards made one very conscious of the figure. And so people started to slim down. I find that a lot of youngsters have bare bones here, which I never saw before."

"Oh, they want you to be thin all right!" says Cynthia Harvey. "They just sort of say, 'Thin, please . . .' However you have to do it, just, 'Thin, please . . .'"

There are no hard and fast standards for ballerinas, no weight and height specifications that schools or companies dictate to their dancers. No one says, "If you're five feet two inches, then you must weigh ninety-eight pounds," and no one says, "The dancer who performs the First Sailor in *Fancy Free* must be this tall and weigh this much." Nevertheless, a consciousness of weight as it affects a dancer's appearance and performance pervades every studio and every rehearsal hall.

Sixteen-year-old Dierdre Carberry, a promising addition to American Ballet Theatre, sums up what every dancer is looking for. "I would just like to stay lean and muscular and have a good body without a lot of body fat."

In some ways, of course, it's easier for dancers than for other people, because they are constantly monitoring the appearance and performance of their bodies. And they have an invaluable tool for doing so: the mirror.

The dieter's best friend—or worst enemy—is her mirror. The mirror is even more accurate than a scale in telling a dieter when she needs to lose weight. Just reading body-weight tables or figuring weight per inches for specific age groups won't give the true picture of which weight is the right one for an individual.

The mirror is also an essential element of a dancer's weight regimen. No bug or cell under a microscope was ever scrutinized by a scientist more intently than dancers scrutinize themselves in the mirror.

A ballet studio is a large, bare room with wooden floors. Usually, the only furnishings are the piano, a chair or two, the wooden barre just about waist-high along the walls and at least one wall with full-length mirrors from one corner to the other.

Every day in class the dancers line up along the barre. As the class progresses, they watch themselves carefully in the mirror, always examining their bodies and judging their execution of various movements and combinations.

In terms of physical exertion, class is very demanding but one of its most important features is this process of self-criticism. Dancers are continuously conducting a visual dissection of their bodies.

The mirror can tell a dancer several things: First, am I executing this step correctly? Is my form all right? Am I doing this gracefully enough? And, how will I look to an audience—like a klutz or a fatso, or like a ballerina?

When a dancer makes the decision to diet and take off a few pounds, it usually comes as a result of that assessment. As every dieter knows well, losing pounds doesn't always mean losing the necessary inches.

Susan Jaffe talks about the difference between what the scale and the mirror say when it comes to losing weight. "Well, I use both when I keep track of my weight. But it's funny, because even when I lost weight last year, I still *looked* heavier than I do now. I looked heavier because I didn't have defined muscles. I wasn't as strong. Even though my weight was a hundred two, the mirror told me I had to be even thinner in order to look thin."

Susan's comment is a typical one. All dancers seem to have an ideal in mind and are busy comparing their mirror images to that mental ideal while they're at work in class or rehearsal.

"We are so visual," explains Cynthia Harvey. "Dance is a visual thing. Most of the time all of us have an image of what we'd like to look like.

"Usually, it's an image of someone else. You know, it really is stupid, because you can't actually change your physicality. You might be able to change the shape of your muscles to a great degree, but the way the muscles are attached to the bone can't be changed all that much."

Christine Redpath stretching in front of the mirror—the dieter's best friend or worst enemy. *(Photo copyright © 1983 by Martha Swope)*

When asked what dancer Cynthia would like to look like, she replies, "The closest is Makarova."

That Cynthia would name Natalia Makarova, the great Russian ballerina, is no surprise. Natasha is tiny and ethereal-looking, and is almost as responsible as Balanchine for promoting ballet's thin look today.

"No, she's not too thin," says Cynthia. "She looks wonderful. She *can* get too thin, but she gives me hope. I saw pictures of her at my age and she was rounder then. But," she sighed, "I don't have the same shaped legs that she has, and I don't ever expect to have those gorgeous feet.

"Patty McBride is another one who has beautiful legs. I love her legs. I could look at them forever."

Having an ideal in mind is all very well for keeping dancers working toward a goal, but each dancer should learn her own strengths and weaknesses so she can play up the one and work to improve the other.

Assessing her own physical characteristics, Cynthia says, "My bone structure is small, so I don't have to get bony to look thin. On the other hand, I can't carry any extra weight. All around I think I should be five pounds thinner than I am. I've been bad," she confesses.

"Everybody's different, though. I don't like to be stereotyped. Too many people try to generalize everything and put it all into one category or another."

"I can't always tell how I look just by looking at myself in the mirror," Fernando Bujones explains, "because I'm used to what I am seeing. I'm not the sort who really worries about my weight unless people start saying a great deal about it. Then maybe I begin to look at myself and rush to a scale.

"It was actually only when I saw photographs of myself that I saw that my face has become less round. Now I see more angles, more sharp edges everywhere—less roundness in the legs."

Fernando, however, seems to be one of the lucky exceptions.

Most dancers say they want to lose three or five pounds. Their self-images always seem to fall short of perfection—that helps keep them motivated. Being surrounded by other dancers in class and rehearsal, hearing them talk about their bodies and their diets, seeing that the successful dancers seem as thin as can be, all of these things work to keep a dancer aware of those few extra pounds. Dancers are so much in tune with their bodies, in fact, that they seem to notice extra ounces where the average person will only notice pounds.

Nonprofessionals can also get caught up in the drive for the "ballerina look." Many ballet classes include both professionals and nonprofessionals, so many students who may not *have* to keep their weight way down are still uncomfortably conscious of weighing more than the others. It may be simply a case of fashion, or what's in vogue, or maybe a romantic view of ballerinas, but it's also something that everyone is faced with, professional and nonprofessional alike: self-doubt.

Isabel Brown describes her daughter Leslie's weight concerns. "Leslie says, 'If I wake up in the morning feeling fat, I *act* fat all day. And if I feel I am thin, then I feel good all day and I *act* thin.' I think that's the key right there." Caught up in the pressure created by that mirror-versus-mental-image, a dancer needs all the positive thinking she can get.

Heather Watts, a principal dancer with the New York City Ballet, has a similar philosophy. "The few times in my life that I've felt heavy, I've decided not to eat so much that day, and then, you know, I eat twice as much. I think it's a very mental thing.

"You watch the young girls in the company struggling with their weight. They think they're fat, and they look at themselves and think they're fat, and all that they think about is how they're fat. They think about food all the time. I think you should fight that kind of thing."

"Some people with a little extra weight, well, it just doesn't make a whole lot of difference," says Peter Fonseca, "but other people can't afford it. Each person is an individual case.

"I can't afford an extra four or five pounds. It makes me look bloated. As soon as I lose the first five pounds, I feel much better. And then I'm not carrying all that extra weight around and it gets easier to perform. You see, it's a matter of getting up to a high-energy level and then being able to function all day long at that energy level without getting pulled down by the extra weight."

Dierdre Carberry uses these simple tests: "You know how your pants fit. You can also tell onstage. The scale is more depressing." How much does Dierdre weigh? "Um, about a hundred."

Now, how can you decide whether or not you need to lose weight? If you own a leotard, you might like to try it the way the dancers do (you can also try it in your underwear):

- Stand in front of a mirror—a three-way mirror is best of all—and examine yourself from many angles.

- Now weigh yourself.

- Make a note of the spots you're not satisfied with—jot them down on a check-list. (For example, your weight might be acceptable in a chart of normal weight ranges for Americans your age, but your observations in the mirror indicate that your proportions are wrong.)

- Try and make it a habit to examine yourself this way every day.

After a week of these examinations compare your visual assessments of your body with the scale weights you wrote down. Very likely you'll be surprised at the results.

If, like many women, your extra weight ends up on your hips and thighs or you are carrying an extra band of fat around your waist, the mirror assessment is telling you to lose those pounds.

Violette Verdy weighing in (be sure to subtract the weight of the
pointe shoes!). (*Photo copyright © 1983 by Martha Swope*)

If your weight falls high in the normal range, and yet your bone structure allows you to carry it with graceful proportion, don't let anyone tell you that you need to lose weight. The idea here is to allow your individual physical characteristics to dictate your weight-control regimen, and not some fashion or some chart or some well-meaning friend.

The decision to lose weight or not to lose weight will have to be your own decision, and that's why an honest self-appraisal must be your first move.

If, after your examination, what you've seen does not look perfect to you, you'll know that you not only need to diet but to exercise as well. In later chapters of this book, the dancers will be outlining the specific weight-loss programs they turn to when the mirror tells them they need to diet.

Below is a chart that was devised at the HEW conference on obesity in 1973, and it lists the USDA recommended body-weight ranges based on height. As an interesting comparison, the heights and weights of six dancers are listed as well.

SUGGESTED BODY WEIGHTS

Range of Acceptable Weight
(Pounds)

Height (Feet-inches)	Men (Pounds)	Women (Pounds)
4'10"		92–119
4'11"		94–122
5'0"		96–125
5'1"		99–128
5'2"	112–141	102–131
5'3"	115–144	105–134
5'4"	118–148	108–138
5'5"	121–152	111–142

Height (Feet-inches)	Men (Pounds)	Women (Pounds)
5'6"	124–156	114–146
5'7"	128–161	118–150
5'8"	132–166	122–154
5'9"	136–170	126–158
5'10"	140–174	130–163
5'11"	144–179	134–168
6'0"	148–184	138–173
6'1"	152–189	
6'2"	156–194	
6'3"	160–199	
6'4"	164–204	

NOTE: Height without shoes; weight without clothes.

SIX SELECTED DANCERS' WEIGHTS

Height (Feet-inches)	Men (Pounds)	Women (Pounds)
5'3"		Natalia Makarova 94
5'4 ¼"		Cynthia Harvey 101–106
5'5"		Susan Jaffe 102
5'7"	Mikhail Baryshnikov 147	
6'0"	Rudolf Nureyev 170	
6'2"	Peter Martins 182	

As you might have expected, the ballerinas maintain weights that are as much as eleven pounds below the minimum weights for their heights. Male dancers, on the other hand, fall well within their appropriate ranges. A generally accepted explanation for that difference is the fact that male dancers carry greater amounts of muscle mass than do their female counterparts.

An average American female should *not* aim for the very low weight of the average ballerina. In the first place, it simply isn't necessary—not for health, well-being or good looks. A ballerina's need to be thinner than thin is the result of her "magnified exposure" onstage, in a rehearsal hall and at the barre. The average woman will probably never be subjected to the same degree of scrutiny and comparison.

Secondly, even with a vigorous exercise program, it's unlikely that the average American woman will burn calories as fast as the dancer will. That could mean that in order to be as thin as a Makarova, she would have to do more dieting than is wise.

Most women will, and *should*, be more than satisfied with reaching a weight that is on the low side of their respective ranges. In fact, with a comfortable weight that is not too difficult to maintain, you will find you have adequate energy and, at the same time, are encouraged to develop healthy eating and exercising habits.

Your goal should be to become *less* obsessed with your weight by making a well-rounded diet and an invigorating physical program so routine that they become a habit and not an unpleasant necessity.

In any case, do not allow your weight to fall below the minimum for your range without checking with your doctor.

As the dancers have said before, however, your weight in pounds should be less important to you than your weight as it looks in the mirror. In other words, what do you think looks good on your body?

When in front of the mirror, remember:

· Look at your body as a whole, carefully assessing your proportions.

· Isolate the problem area or areas.

· Monitor your progress as you work to lose weight.

Most important of all, remember these three "be's":

· Be realistic!

· Be truthful!

· Be patient!

CHAPTER TWO

The Dancers' Secret

No diet, no exercise plan, will do you any good unless you have the discipline to make them work for you. Dancers have that discipline.

Before exploring the specific ways in which dancers diet, we need to see how they sustain that discipline, how they summon the necessary willpower to lose the weight and keep it off.

In theory, anyone can lose weight simply by expending more calories than he or she takes in. But what motivates a dancer to strictly limit eating while putting out tremendous amounts of energy is desire and self-discipline.

That's it. That is the dancers' secret in a nutshell.

With discipline you can accomplish just about anything, and dancers are trained in discipline from the time they put on their first dancing shoes. Discipline is what keeps you at a difficult or unpleasant job, like dieting, no matter what excuses your inner voice can think up to try and put it off.

And once you have discipline, you never really lose it.

All dancers have self-discipline, some more than others of course, because without it you just can't expect to succeed in the ballet world. In talking with dancers about how discipline helps them in weight-loss and exercise programs, it was equally fascinating to learn how they apply discipline to nearly all parts of their lives.

Muriel Stuart is a beautiful eighty-year-old, yet she doesn't feel, or act, her age. "I can rush up the stairs . . . up and down.

Good heavens, I don't have to tell you how old I am. I'm an old lady, but I don't feel it. I have been very active the past few years.

"I think that it is the exercise and the discipline. You have to have both. You can't overdo it and you can't underdo it! You have to be rational about it, of course.

"Now all I do is a small exercise in the morning. I never start the day without it. As you know, in my day there were no such things as vitamins. At least, I didn't know about them. But here I am! I think that you have to keep active and keep your body going."

What would she recommend for dancers and non-dancers? "Walk as much as possible instead of always taking a bus or taxi. I mean, I'm an old woman now, but I don't feel so."

My own key thing has always been: *Keep moving!* It is thrilling to hear Muriel say nearly the same thing and be able to prove how beneficial it is! At an age when most women restrict their activity, here is Muriel rushing up and down her stairs and religiously following her exercise regimen every morning.

Such devotion to duty is common among dancers. Marika Molnar speculates that dancers are able to push themselves regularly beyond normal limits.

"Most dancers do," says Marika. "Our bodies have a lot of potential, and rarely does anyone tax himself to the ultimate limit, yet dancers spend a lot of time doing just that."

"From day to day, the body has continually to start at the beginning and then progress to a point where it can then go on and do fantastic things or whatever the choreographer wishes to be done. I think that it is an essential part of building healthy dancers. It is such a simple and basic concept: the repeated, daily usage of the part of your body that needs work. You keep the body in tune that way."

Most dancers recommend the "day to day" approach as the secret to acquiring discipline.

"Everybody should exercise every day. It is easier to do that when there's some sort of discipline involved," says Merrill Ashley, a starring ballerina with the New York City Ballet. She confesses that she needs some help with discipline. Like many others, she gets it by going to training sessions.

"I am terrible working by myself," says Merrill. "I need to go somewhere and have someone give me the exercises. If I have to do them on my own, they don't get done.

"But I think that the basic thing is to do exercises every day. That's the most important thing. It gets easier when you do it every day, especially when it's in a disciplined atmosphere. If you have all sorts of things distracting you, how are you ever going to get it done? And a change in atmosphere can also help. I would love to go out in the park and run around, just for the change of atmosphere."

What Merrill is saying here is that if you think you don't have the self-discipline to follow an every-day regimen of exercising, *there are ways to go out and get it.* Joining a class or signing up for a training course, doing it with a friend or just varying a routine, may be all you need to motivate yourself.

Dancers have an advantage. They learn discipline and motivation from the first ballet lessons, through a carefully structured progression of instruction. Later, in the company, the dancers discover that even more discipline is required of every member, from the newest girl in the corps to the most experienced star.

From the time when a dancer is very young, the routine of working the body to exhaustion becomes a matter of course. And, by working harder all the time, dancers eventually teach their bodies to accept a level of pain and exhaustion that the average person would never put up with.

It's said that the most famous ballerina of the nineteenth century, Marie Taglioni (1804–1884), was forced to work so hard as a student that she would regularly collapse in tears from exhaustion. Her father, the renowned dancer Filippo Taglioni, was unmoved by both her tears and her bloody feet, and forced her to

Merrill Ashley of NYCB with Victor Castelli in Balanchine's *Symphony in Three Movements.* *(Photo copyright © 1983 by Martha Swope)*

continue working until she became one of the greatest dancers in history, technically and artistically. This may sound like a fanciful story, but every generation of ballet students reports the same grueling trials. At first it may be a course that's enforced by parents or teachers, but eventually it becomes a form of self-discipline.

"Hard work is what you're supposed to do if you want to become a dancer," explains Peter Fonseca. "Sometimes you might feel resentful that you've worked so hard. What you end up figuring out, though, is that you really do like to work that hard, and if you didn't work that hard you would probably be just miserable."

Other dancers also tell about working so hard that they simply fall asleep in class or in the dressing rooms. But dancers seem to agree that hard work is part of their training and that they aren't really happy unless they're active.

Does it sound as if guilt plays a big part in a dancer's self-discipline? That's probably true. If you're not in class with the rest of your friends and classmates, you feel you're letting not only yourself down, but the others as well.

It's sometimes so hard to do what you know you should that you will want to find any excuse to avoid it. *But you don't avoid it.* By forcing yourself to go on, you get as used to working hard, or dieting, as you are used to brushing your teeth. And that's just about the best way to maintain discipline.

Naturally, many ballet students fall by the wayside through the years, but those who become professionals maintain the daily drill and routine all through their lives. And even those who don't pursue a ballet career beyond childhood have often absorbed the valuable habits of discipline ballet instills. That's not to say, however, that we can coast along without reinforcing that habit.

Mel Tomlinson warns, "You can never take it for granted, because if you do, it's usually the first thing to go."

Maybe it's the fact that dancers are more or less on display most of the time that motivates them. After all, they're not sitting behind a desk or doing business over the telephone all day, and they're expected to look their best or else.

Most find it natural to apply discipline to dancing, but how do dancers go about using it for other purposes, like dieting?

"So much of it is mental. You discipline your mind," says Peter Fonseca of the way he applies discipline to his everyday life.

"I find that I can do whatever I want as long as I *train* myself to do it. I have to bring myself along in a methodical way, so that my body has the time to absorb what then become habits. If I can make it a habit, then it's easier.

"If I don't make it a habit, it becomes a constant question, 'Should I or shouldn't I?' It becomes a fight and you end up spending all your time struggling to decide when you should or should not do something. But if it's a habit, it becomes easy."

Methodically training your mind and body to do what's required without questioning is always worthwhile. If you're not constantly fighting yourself, you've got a lot more time to worry about more important things.

Dancers also find that self-discipline is essential in times of stress or injury. Merrill Ashley describes her ability to perform, even with illness or pain.

"I have a fairly high threshold of pain. Somehow when I'm dancing, I don't feel pain very much. I can block it out most of the time. Like the other day with my hip, when it was at its very worst. It was the day of an important premiere. You say to yourself, 'It's an important night and I am going to do it, period.' I know what steps are going to hurt, and I just brace myself for those and forget about it."

Other dancers discussed the phenomenon of forgetting everything else in the euphoria, or terror, of a performance. "It is funny sometimes," says Fernando Bujones. "I've had a wobbly or

Fernando Bujones of ABT in *Konservatoriet*, choreographed by
Auguste Bournonville. *(Photo copyright © 1983 by Martha Swope)*

uncomfortable stomach before a performance, but my body has always been able to throw it off, to reject it just at the moment I'm going out onstage."

What applies to stomach aches and injuries can also apply to stamina and endurance.

"Dancers never surprise me in the amount of endurance they can produce," says Peter Fonseca. "We are used to coping with stress and strain on a daily basis. After all, you put your body on a schedule where you demand eight hours of full out exertion during the day."

Of course, stamina varies from dancer to dancer, and yet a dancer without endurance cannot survive in the competitive world of ballet. Training helps, but a great deal of it is simply a matter of self-discipline.

Part of the artistry of ballet dancing comes in making something incredibly difficult look incredibly easy. Making it through an evening's performance and still looking as fresh and strong at the final curtain as you did when the curtain first rose takes endurance and willpower.

Beautiful Suzanne Farrell, star of the New York City Ballet, has long had a reputation for unlimited reserves of stamina and strength. However, she swears that it often takes all of her self-discipline to summon it up.

"I ran into a woman the other day who said, 'You aren't as young as you used to be.' I said, 'Well, it's true that I'm not as young as I used to be, but I feel younger than I did before.' I have the same amount of stamina, if not more. I have a strong mind, although I'm not the kind of person who can just put her mind to it and have more stamina.

"Somebody gave me that stigma that I never get tired, and I think some of it is just a matter of being comfortable. I just assumed I wasn't allowed to get tired. I do get tired though. But people say, 'You never get tired!,' so I don't let them know that I'm dying."

Suzanne continues, "I feel that I know my body pretty well.

Whenever I feel something is wrong, I still continue to work. I seem to do better, everything falls into place if I work. It doesn't mean I have to kill myself, but it does mean I have to exercise and then my whole system works better.

"People don't really realize that dancing is an all-day affair in some form or another, even if you aren't working. You know, how can you really, really relax if you have to pull yourself together and get out in front of two or three thousand people?"

Stamina, discipline, motivation . . . what makes a dancer keep with it?

"It is a very special life," says Suzanne. "I know it's what I want."

Now, how does all of this apply to dieting? Dancers say that the first battle in weight loss is always the battle of the mental attitude. Calling on skills of self-discipline is one of the only ways to win the battle.

Martine van Hamel is one of American Ballet Theatre's star ballerinas, but she too has had her own struggle to lose weight.

"While I was growing up, in my teens, my family always ate well. There was never a consciousness of what we were doing or what I was eating. For a long time at one stage I tended to accept that I was overweight.

"To change that, I just had to work very hard. Now I think that I'm finally happier when I'm working and dancing. I think that most of the time when I wasn't working in Manhattan, my revenge was to become fat. I had to get past that stage. Finally, I started to work and dance more. Then it just naturally comes off . . . when my mind is ready."

Many dancers agree that losing weight is much easier at certain times than it is at others, and it has everything to do with being in the right mental state at the right time. But each has gone through times when nothing seems to work.

"I am very ready to work hard, rehearse hard and perform hard," says Merrill Ashley. "But I am *not* ready to diet hard! I just am not. It's as if my willpower is at an end—it must be somewhere else!

"If I start eating early in the day, I want to keep eating all day long. It's as if . . . I don't know, maybe a mental problem, but eating early just seems to stimulate my desire to eat constantly. Then, of course, I'm heavier and I feel full when it comes time to perform.

"I try to wait somehow until after class to eat something. Then after class I don't feel so hungry usually. I feel I have plenty of energy in the morning. I don't feel hungry and I don't feel tired," she explains.

A good work-out in class does often seem to help curb an appetite. Many dancers don't feel the need for much more than a small lunch when they're in the middle of a working day. Merrill's tip about not eating in the morning can be useful, although many other dancers say they need something at breakfast to start the day on.

Finding the right mental attitude is really often a matter of knowing your own body, which we discussed in the last chapter. Assessing your own weaknesses and strengths helps you learn what will work in getting your mind prepared for a diet. Every dancer relies on something unique to become mentally committed to staying thin—something that's been tried and found true for him or her.

Some might set a deadline: "I must lose five pounds by the time of the season's first rehearsal." Others make a commitment with a friend: "If you'll quit smoking, I'll lose ten pounds!" There are dancers who just try to stay out of the house, away from the refrigerator, or who will keep the cupboards absolutely bare in order to avoid temptation.

One effective way to keep a lasting commitment to the diet is to set some new ground rules for yourself. Ask yourself, "Why do I eat when I'm not hungry? Why do I think about food when it's not mealtime? Why do I think I have to eat and drink in order to be sociable? Am I really even *thinking* about what I'm putting in my mouth?" Once you've started to realize that you eat for any number of reasons other than the fact that you feel hungry, you can set your own rules about eating.

Peter Fonseca has done just that with the personal philosophy he calls "minimalism," a philosophy he derived independently, but which closely conforms to behavior modification, a psychological tool for altering habits. By relating his eating to all other facets of his daily life, he can get a more realistic attitude toward dieting. But "minimalism," for Peter, applies to all of his activities and makes him that much more conscientious in setting goals and working toward them.

"So many people just consume and consume and don't put anything out. I think the answer is to be absolutely minimal in what you take in and prolific in what you put out," he explains.

"That means you have to draw a lot more on your energy and spirit and creativity to produce something, rather than just use up all of the resources around you without producing anything.

"It's a question of everybody always wanting more of this, that and the other, and when they want something, you have to take from one to give to the other. People just don't have any sense of how little they need to get by."

Working, dancing and staying in top form are important, not only to dancers who want to watch their weight but also to dancers who don't need to watch their weight, the lucky ones like Fernando Bujones or New York City Ballet star Patricia McBride.

Patty and her husband, Jean-Pierre Bonnefous, laughed when I said that I thought Patty's secret had to be 98 percent talent and 2 percent pasta. "I can eat anything, I just enjoy pasta!" Patty says.

But for the rest of us, dieting is a necessary evil, and dancers look for any way they can to get it done. Part of the secret is to enjoy what you're doing, and that, naturally, makes it easier to discipline yourself into staying thin. It's essential that the rewards of a dancer's life remain at least as great as its demands.

As Suzanne says: "You have to enjoy what you are doing; everything goes together much better then."

Emotional attitudes play a big part in any weight-loss success, and in any kind of success for that matter. One might be self-critical or doubtful about one's appearance, providing the motivation to lose weight, but a positive attitude is essential in bolstering willpower and disciplining dieting habits.

"What you have to do as far as I am concerned," comments Muriel Stuart, "is keep your emotional stability. That's the most important thing. Once you have control of your emotions, you can begin to compare and discover what is really great and successful."

Ideally, of course, you should be able to look at yourself, want to lose weight and then be able to go out and do it. But most of us are like Merrill Ashley and need help motivating ourselves to begin, and sticking to whatever has to be done.

Based on the experiences of the dancers, here are some suggestions that can help you reach the goals you've set for yourself:

- Take the time to ask yourself just exactly why you want to lose weight. Write down your reasons, even the silly ones, so that all through your diet you will be able to remind yourself of the motives that got you started.

- Make commitments to yourself about how many pounds you need to lose, or how long you can take to lose them, or what level of exercise you plan to achieve. *Record* those commitments in writing or with a friend. Otherwise, it's far too easy to forget or ignore those commitments when the going gets tough.

- Make your weight-loss activities habit-forming. If we can brush our teeth every morning out of habit, why

Suzanne Farrell and Jacques D'Amboise of NYCB in *Meditations* by George Balanchine. *(Photo copyright © 1983 by Martha Swope)*

can't we see to our daily exercise out of habit? Why can't we pass by the bread or the dessert out of habit, instead of helping ourselves to them just because that's what we've always done? You make something a habit by forcing yourself to repeat it *every day*. Nothing less than that will change your bad habits into good ones.

· If you can't find the willpower within yourself, take a look around you. Spend your hard-earned money on a health-club membership or a series of exercise classes, and then make sure you get your money's worth out of it. Persuade a friend to join you, and rely on each other to provide guilt, compulsion, bribery, companionship or whatever it takes to motivate you.

· Pretend that all of your success in life depends on your ability to diet for just today. Then do the same thing tomorrow, and so on. Set realistic, feasible goals for yourself—and then make sure you achieve them.

· Don't be negative. Don't underestimate yourself. You've accomplished lots of difficult things in your life, and sticking to a diet can certainly be one of them. Enjoy the task as a challenge, and don't let past failures intimidate you this time.

· Keep trying. Don't let one careless meal, or one thoughtless binge, or a missed deadline, or a slow weight loss knock all of your hard work out the window. One slip should not be the excuse for you to sink back into old, bad habits.

CHAPTER THREE
The Dancers' Diet

Through the interviews with the dancers, it became apparent that no one has a "magic diet." There's no one type of food, like grapefruit or cottage cheese, that all swear by, nor is there an extreme method, like fasting, that any dancer would say works very well or even that a dancer would recommend to others.

Those of us who've tried one or another of the "quick-weight-loss" plans that seem to crop up every other month have found that these diets are just not the answer. Among the reasons dancers cite are:

- Crash diets may work for a while, but they can't solve anybody's weight problems permanently.

- After you've gone off a crash diet, you'll usually gain back the pounds you lost, and sometimes more.

- They're not good for your health over an extended period of time.

- They've been known to cause loss of energy, loss of stamina or emotional changes.

Dancers agree that dieting successfully takes time and a real effort of will. Any diet plan that promises permanent results in a few days or weeks is a diet plan to be skeptical of.

That isn't to say that dancers haven't tried exotic diets to take off a few pounds or to bolster flagging willpower (Chapter Six takes a look at some of the odder and funnier attempts dancers have made to lose weight). Basically, however, a diet you can live with and lose by is a diet that follows the advice of Susan Jaffe, who says, "Eat a well-rounded diet," and Peter Fonseca, who adds, "But be minimal about it."

What most dancers have in common is a *philosophy* about dieting. It's a philosophy that seems to work for a group of people who need to be the thinnest and the fittest, and it's a philosophy that can work for just about everyone else as well.

This philosophy, or attitude, can be broken down into three simple rules. Each rule is important, but, *in order to lose weight and keep it off, you must follow all three rules*:

> *Rule Number One*: Keep your food intake to a healthy minimum.

> *Rule Number Two*: Eat a well-rounded, balanced variety of foods.

> *Rule Number Three*: Make exercise and physical activity a part of your diet.

For years, every dieter has been taught, retaught and further impressed with the fundamental principle behind the relationship of calorie consumption to weight loss or gain. There is probably very little any ballerina can tell you that will shed more light on the subject. But let's go through it just one time:

The energy derived from food is measured as calories. Very basically, for every action your body takes, and that includes simply breathing as well as a dancer's pirouette, your body burns some of the food you've been feeding it. Typing at a desk for an hour burns 80 to 100 calories, while dancing for an hour burns more than 350.

It's easy to see that a dancer can eat a cup of ice cream, which contains approximately 330 calories, and burn it off in less than an hour of hard work at the barre. The office worker, also hard at work, needs more than three hours to "pay" for that same delicious cup of ice cream.

The good news is that no matter what you're doing, even sleeping, your body is burning calories. The bad news is that the average American eats more than he or she needs to meet the average body's energy requirements, and that extra food energy is then stored as fat.

The basic principle of weight control—and the experiences of dancers bear this out—is that when you raise your activity level (burning more calories) and reduce your food intake (taking in fewer calories), your body will burn the fat it is storing, the very fat you'd like to get rid of.

No other combination—not protein, carbohydrates, grapefruit or appetite suppressors—will help you stay slim in the long run if you don't cut down on what you eat at the same time you're getting out there and becoming more active.

It sounds so simple, doesn't it? Theoretically, if you stay on a twelve-hundred-calorie-a-day diet while burning seventeen hundred calories a day (not a very strenuous regimen), you will burn an extra thirty-five hundred calories every week. Result: You'll be losing one pound a week. Four months later you'll have taken off sixteen pounds. If that's all you needed to lose, you can then add something extra to your diet to raise it to the seventeen-hundred-calorie-a-day level, meanwhile maintaining your by then habitual seventeen-hundred-calorie-a-day activities, and you have your perfectly balanced, stay-slim diet plan.

Hundreds of dancers and millions of dieters, however, know that it isn't that simple. If it were, a book on how dancers maintain their figures would be of no interest to anyone.

The body, of course, is a very complicated piece of machinery and, as any ballet master or choreographer will tell you, bodies resist all efforts to stereotype them.

Whenever you change your eating and exercise habits, your

body's metabolism changes as well. Because your body is adjusting to the new state of things, you'll often find that there is a certain level below which it is frustratingly difficult to reduce. That level varies from person to person.

When you reach that frustrating level on your diet, it might be tempting to eat less, or even to starve yourself in order to reduce. It's a time when those strange crash-diet programs look pretty alluring. After all, you reason, you won't be on it for very long.

The best advice, however, is, "Don't!"

It's widely accepted these days that crazy diets, even if you're absolutely, positively guaranteed to lose ten pounds in just seven days, simply don't work. Most people who do lose those ten pounds very quickly will soon gain them back again, and will often gain a few more pounds in the bargain.

Until you've changed your ways for good, and for the better, you're not going to lose weight successfully. Nearly every dancer interviewed emphasizes that a sensible change in eating habits, a change that ensures adequate nutrition even while it cuts back on calories, is the only way to take weight off and keep it off.

That's why all three weight-loss rules of the Dancers' Diet must be followed in order to work for you.

If you're going to jog five miles every day but still raid the refrigerator every evening, your cardiovascular health might improve even though your waistline won't. If you're going to cut down on what you eat and join an aerobics class, but don't eat a well-balanced three meals a day, you'll find yourself off the diet with headaches, dizziness and fatigue. And if you keep to a sensible, balanced diet plan while restricting your activity to television-dial flipping, you'll find yourself, after a torturously long time, as flabby as you used to be fat, and just as lethargic too.

In other words, each of the three vital points of the Dancers' Diet Plan plays a part in helping you lose weight and then keep it off for good.

Keeping it off for good should be as big a goal to you as your goal of losing five or ten or fifty pounds. And a short-range crash diet won't help you change your habits for the better. After all, three cups of cottage cheese and a grapefruit every day might take off a few pounds, but who in the world can stick to a diet like that for very long? Even if you *could* stick to it, you wouldn't be good for much after a few days—you certainly wouldn't be able to keep up in a ballet class or dance very capably in an evening's performance.

It's so much better for you if you would say to yourself:

"All of these dancers can cut down on what they eat and still outperform anyone else. If they can do it, I know I can too. Starting right now, I'm going to watch what I eat. I'm going to make my portions smaller, and I'm going to start leaving food on my plate. I'm going to cut out 'empty' calories and high-calorie extras. My three meals will be well balanced and nutritious. Best of all, I'm going to begin an exercise program, and I'll start right now with a good brisk walk!"

Rule Number One: Keep Your Food Intake to a Healthy Minimum

Only you can know what minimum level of food intake is one that's healthy and practical for you.

However, dieting almost always means cutting way down on sugars and fats. It means cutting down on portions at meals, cutting out the snacks, the extra cocktail, the second helping, and the extra cream in your coffee.

Some people can even cut down to two meals a day, but I find that I just can't go through the day without eating. I am happier with myself and my diet if I eat three small meals during the day.

Cynthia Harvey of ABT aloft in a "stag leap" in *La Bayadère*, staged by Natalia Makarova after Marius Petipa. *(Photo copyright © 1983 by Martha Swope)*

Cynthia Harvey agrees. "Most of the time, I really don't eat three meals a day, although I know that when I do I'm better off. In fact, I went to a nutritionist who told me I'd be better off eating six tiny meals a day for my metabolism . . . to keep my protein level up—tiny, tiny, not even meals exactly."

Several dancers said they'd rather eat several very small meals if they could, but schedules and appointments usually interfere. Like most people, dancers have to fit meals into their schedules, so they usually can't be as creative as they'd like about when and what they eat.

Merrill Ashley finds that breakfast seems to wake up her appetite, and she diets more easily if she skips a morning meal. Others warn against missing that first meal of the day.

"I still think the morning meals are very important," advises Marika Molnar. "Not that you have to eat a whole meal, but maybe half a grapefruit and a piece of toast. Just something to start the day."

Peter Fonseca also feels breakfast is necessary, and he finds it easier to cut out a midday meal when he's watching his weight. "My own diet, the one that works for me, is that I eat a minimal breakfast: fruit, juice and coffee with cream, and sometimes I'll include a slice of bread depending on how much I ate the night before or how late.

"Then I don't eat anything all day. If I have to perform until late at night and don't have a chance to fit in dinner, I will have coffee and fruit before the performance and then a light dinner afterward. If I don't have to dance, then I'll just eat a good dinner.

"What I try to do is get used to functioning at a high energy level all day long with as little eating as possible. I mean, within reason of course, not trying to starve myself. If I can get to the point where I'm used to smaller amounts of food, it gets easier. At first, getting through a whole day is the hard part."

Several dancers explained that getting used to smaller portions was something to work toward. Not only does it help in losing weight, but it also sets you up properly for the habit of eating sensibly for a life-long maintenance diet.

Susan Jaffe's regimen goes like this: "I usually don't have time for lunch. For dinner I'll have an apple and a quarter of a pound of chicken or tuna or egg salad with some crackers. With a cup of coffee afterward, I'm fine. I feel good and it gives me energy.

"Most people say, 'Oh, my God, only a quarter of a pound?' but it's enough if you sit down and you really eat it. If you taste what you're eating and properly chew your food, you won't have to throw down five hamburgers in order to feel satisfied.

"That's how I taught myself to eat again after I lost all that weight."

Another dancer who reports that a strict diet helped her re-adjust her eating habits is Merrill Ashley. "I relaxed a little bit [after dieting], but the weight hasn't come back on. I feel it helped build some good habits. I saw how I could be satisfied with a smaller amount of food."

Did Merrill count calories on her diet?

"Well, you know, I do and I don't. Recently, I have been counting, because I'd gotten heavy and I just couldn't get it off. I finally just started to count calories and that was the only way I started to lose weight.

"I think it was because it just made me more *aware* of the number of calories I was eating. Because otherwise, somehow, it was too easy to eat a little more and not even be conscious of it."

Very few dancers indicated that they counted calories, in a weight-loss diet. But nearly all of them revealed in their inter-views that they have a knowledge of the relative caloric values of most foods and employ that knowledge in watching what and how much they eat.

It isn't necessary to sit down with a calorie counter, but it can help to consider calories when planning daily meals. One can be very systematic about it, writing down what food to eat that day and then crossing things off as they are eaten. That way, you can eat just what you had planned and no more. But not everyone needs to be that organized.

Darci Kistler, a young principal with the New York City Ballet, explains her attitude toward calorie counting. "No [she doesn't count calories], and I've never gone on a diet, either. I just cut out sweets and I can lose weight."

Madame Danilova echoes the same idea when she explains why she never eats ice cream. "It is very fattening. If I don't eat it, I forget how it tastes and I don't miss it. Ice cream is very, very fattening."

Being aware of how many calories are in the things we eat is so important that it should become second nature. That only comes, however, when you've familiarized yourself with various diet plans, the relative caloric values of specific food portions and a comparison of food substitutes.

For example, reading and using diet menus that are broken down into calories can help you budget your calories for a reducing diet and, later, for a maintenance diet. Buy one of those paperback or pocket-sized books that list specific caloric values, and use it when planning a menu or after eating a meal in a restaurant or at a friend's. You can also use such a guide to compare substitutes—like one scoop of double chocolate fudge ice cream (about 180 calories) versus a nice, sensible peach (35 calories); or a big glob of creamy salad dressing (about 75 calories) versus a squirt of lemon juice and a few fresh herbs (about 1 calorie!).

Start your diet systematically. Write down everything you eat and be truthful about portions. Then figure out how many calories you've consumed, using your guide. For the average American, a twelve-hundred to sixteen-hundred-calorie-a-day diet is considered a safe, slow reducing diet.

You'll gradually learn to budget your calories to stay in that range. If you take a slice of bread with your dinner one night and add a pat of butter to it (about 145 calories), you will probably

Darci Kistler and Ib Andersen of NYCB in *Histoire du Soldat,* choreographed by Peter Martins. *(Photo copyright © 1983 by Martha Swope)*

have to forgo that bowl of raspberry sherbet you'd promised yourself (about 120 calories).

Counting calories is a very good way to examine the priorities
of what you enjoy eating.

Rule Number Two: Eat a Well-rounded, Balanced Variety of Foods

In the crazy, competitive world of ballet, you might think that
the first thing to fall by the wayside would be a dancer's perspective on nutrition.

Not true! Dancers, especially those who have been successful
dieters, have a keen appreciation for nutritious eating. While
everyone has a story to tell about a nameless young dancer who
starves herself, or who subsists on granola cookies, or who goes
on an ice-cream-only diet, any dancer who has gotten through
an exhausting ballet season will emphasize the importance of a
well-balanced diet.

Dierdre Carberry was ABT's youngest member when she
joined the company at the age of fourteen, and yet she speaks
seriously about healthy eating habits. "When you are a dancer,
you don't tend to go out to every vending machine and buy
junk. You buy raisins or juice or lots of other healthy things that
are good for your body, to keep it in good shape for performing
and to keep your energy level going."

That such a young ballerina knows the beneficial influence of
a proper diet is indicative of dancers' generally healthy attitudes.
But regardless of age or experience, dancers on the whole are
more aware of and more careful about nutrition than they are
given credit for.

Edward Villella, one of America's greatest male dancers, explains his own approach to nutritious eating. "Well, what I try to do is simply listen to my body, from both the muscular and the control point of view. I just try to eat what I feel my body is demanding, basically a high-protein, balanced diet. But fortunately, I was brought up with balanced diets."

Asked what she would advise young dancers about nutrition and eating habits, Madame Danilova declares, "Well, that is difficult. I think young dancers are very conscious about what they eat, but I also think that they should eat well . . . eat properly.

"I don't believe you should eat all of this salad. Have a nice piece of fish too. You know a lot of them deprive themselves too completely. That is no good.

"After all, you have to feed the machine. Yes, a balanced diet is important. Some deprive themselves completely—out with sugar, out with butter. But that's no good. You must eat for the machine!"

Pursuing the subject, Marika Molnar discusses what nutrients a dancer needs to look for in balancing her diet. For example, what does a dancer need for energy?

"You are constantly storing energy, but the only thing that you don't store in your body is protein. Your body constantly needs proteins and you always need to replace your supply of proteins.

"Protein is important for the synthesis of tissues. The nervous system needs it to keep itself intact, and tissues in the body need protein to grow healthy and to help heal themselves in case of injury. I believe that protein is an essential food for dancers, and for anyone who taxes his body to the limits that dancers do.

"I would say that a dancer should eat a high-protein diet, and then limited amounts of fat and maybe just a little more carbohydrates, because they are really the better energy food.

"You find protein in meat, eggs and certain vegetables. But you should also realize that proteins and carbohydrates are com-

Madame Alexandra Danilova, prima ballerina assoluta and revered teacher at the School of American Ballet, has been heard to say, "I find lunch demoralizing." She is shown here with Patricia McBride and Helgi Tomasson of NYCB. *(Photo copyright © 1983 by Martha Swope)*

plex things. You can't limit your diet to only one type of food or you will be getting only one kind of protein. The best thing to do is get a list of protein foods, carbohydrate foods and fat foods, and from them, mix and match to come up with a complete and balanced diet.

"Nutrition and food for dancers is an area that, eventually, will have to be further explored," Marika continues. "For the most part—and I'm not saying every single one of them—dancers don't eat nutritiously. If they only knew what to eat, which foods would not increase their weight but would increase their energy levels, it would make all the difference. I am trying to help by putting up posters in the office that deal with calorie intake and high-energy foods and things like that. But I think it is something that should be taught in schools."

Certainly, nutrition should be a part of the training given every professional dancer.

"In this country," says Edward Villella, "we are not taken care of the way a state school or theater takes care of its dancers. Because of that, we have to look out for ourselves and, in a way, I think it's very beneficial only in that it makes you more aware [of how to take care of yourself]."

Fernando Bujones feels strongly about the importance of a diet with variety. "If you eat one specific diet, it's bad. I mix what I eat. I never allow the body to grab at one thing, do you understand? If my body is ready to grab at one thing, if I crave one thing or another, then I feed it something else. A mixture of everything, that's what my body is. And I think that's a good approach."

"You can't overdo one thing," agrees Susan Jaffe. "You can't eat just one thing and not have any other kind of food. I try to eat as well rounded a diet as possible, because that is the healthiest diet. I also take vitamins."

That is one of the most useful pieces of advice dancers offer: Don't limit your diet to one or two foods.

First of all, a strictly limited diet can lead to serious nutritional deficiencies and lasting physical harm. Secondly, the monotony of a limited diet sabotages your weight-loss plans by making it increasingly difficult to stick to the diet.

Finally, you'll find it difficult, if not impossible, to maintain a high activity level when you've limited your nutrition to one or two incomplete menus. For a dancer, this drawback alone is enough to cancel all the benefits of a restricted or "crash" diet.

Peter Fonseca offers the reasons he stays away from extreme diet methods. "I can't diet if I get neurotic about it and say that I can only have cottage cheese and fruit. My own diet is just to eat normally so that I don't get neurotic about missing food. And then I find it easier to cope with the whole situation of being on a diet."

Another dancer who places great importance on healthy eating habits is Cynthia Harvey. She explains that it was her first ballet teacher in California who taught her to be careful about diet and nutrition. "She taught me more about nutrition and physicality than anybody. They don't do that in the big schools."

Cynthia went on to describe her own special diet method. "I know that what works for me is eating a balanced diet. I just can't, you know, cut out everything. The first thing I try to watch is what carbohydrates I'm eating. I don't eat a lot of sugar, for example. (Although I love ice cream—my idea of a celebration is having a bowl of ice cream.) But I try to cut down on bread and dairy products.

"I'll have my main carbohydrate in the morning. Lately it's been just a bowl of cereal."

A life of ballet training will change anybody's approach to eating and dieting. While dancers might seem paranoid about calories, they have still acquired a valuable consciousness about the right way to eat and exercise. As Eddie Villella says, no one but the dancers themselves will watch out for dancers.

If it teaches nothing else, a career in ballet teaches dancers to

Cynthia Harvey ready to feast on some garden products. (*Photo copyright © 1983 by James J. Camner*)

pay attention to the needs of their bodies, and to be *aware* of the vital importance of diet and health.

In summing up the principles of nutritious eating habits, dancers recommend the following:

· Eat a balanced and varied selection of foods.

· Be sure to fuel the machine.

· Be flexible about your diet.

Rule Number Three: Make Exercise and Physical Activity a Part of Your Diet

An all-important recommendation to anyone interested in losing weight and in feeling fit would be to perform some sort of exercise or physical activity for *at least one half-hour every day.*

Frankly, dancers can't understand how anyone can get through the day without at least that much activity. Many say that they have to be active from morning to night or they find themselves simply squirming from inactivity. Dancers never stop moving.

Fernando Bujones says, "If I don't dance, I have to be moving. So when I'm not dancing, I find I am walking to places, and sometimes, even spontaneously, even if I'm not late, my body begins to pick up a pace and I find myself jogging or running."

Of course, the intensity or the type of activity you take up will depend on you. If you've never been one to take part in sports or exercise, or your health precludes any strenuous exercise, why don't you start with a half-hour walk? Or, if you're active by nature, why don't you set yourself a series of goals that will tax and improve your stamina gradually and measurably?

It's harder for people whose lives do not revolve around physical activity. To be fair, dancers have an advantage. They're constantly in motion: jumping, stretching, spinning around. Ballet class is strenuous and invigorating, and many dancers take at least a couple of classes every day. In addition, there are workouts in gymnasiums or swimming pools, dancers walk where they need to go instead of riding, and, of course, on the night of a performance, they're out there dancing into the late hours.

All that activity is bound to burn up a few calories!

Working eight hours at a desk may not present many opportunities to exercise, but everyone has some time to do what he or she likes. It may seem difficult, but surely you can always find a half-hour to spare for your own well-being.

Think of it this way: The calories you'll burn in thirty minutes of walking, jogging, exercise class, tennis or racquetball mean you won't have to torture yourself with starvation diets in order to lose weight or keep a trim figure.

If your half-hour a day is as much a part of your diet as melba toast, yogurt and green salads, you won't resent "losing" the time you might otherwise spend in front of the television.

Dancers agree unanimously about the benefits of a more active life. "Exercise, exactly," is how Mel Tomlinson says it. "We're in the public eye and have to maintain the right appearance. The public is always aware of how we look. Exercise has a great deal to do with looking good. I think it helps our circulation, and that also makes us appear healthy and strong."

When asked which element of a dancer's regimen she would prescribe for the general public, Patty McBride answers, "Just exercise, really. Good exercise is good for everyone. And it's also not sitting, you know. Even just walking, staying mobile, doing anything. I don't sit around a lot."

Jean-Pierre Bonnefous joins in: "Don't you think also, Pat, that some people, because they are over twenty years old, start to feel a little bit older? Dancers have always stayed young, mentally and physically, more than other people seem to. Maybe it's

Jean-Pierre Bonnefous in *Four Bagatelles* by Jerome Robbins. *(Photo copyright © 1983 by Martha Swope)*

because they are doing so much physically that they feel very young.

"Sometimes people feel that exercise is not for them any longer—because they say they're too old or have too many other things to do. I think a lot of people don't realize that they need to have the heart working well in order to feel young and fit.

"Bicycling, jogging or whatever, if they don't do that every day, they can't get started very well. They drink a cup of coffee and try and wake up, but their bodies are just not ready. They never know exactly when their bodies are awake. So they take a nap at the end of the day.

"I think exercise can help people feel better mentally, as well as physically. I think too many people give up perhaps."

Other dancers give similar advice. Asked what he considers a key part of maintaining his health and energy, Jacques D'Amboise, one of America's most famous male dancers, answers, "To fill the days with work. To fill the days with physical activity, and then everything balances out.

"There is no time to stop and eat, and you work so hard that you're not that hungry. And the most important thing to do, the first thing in the morning, is to exercise vigorously and long."

No dancer has to force himself to be active—his body demands it. Dancers know that physical activity doesn't make you more tired—an active day gives you more energy, makes you feel more alive!

The benefits of exercise are almost too many to be listed here. Of most interest to dieters, however, is the marvelous fact that exercise tends to subdue an appetite, not stimulate it. Many dancers report that when forced by injury, illness or vacation to curtail their physical activity, they find themselves hungrier and more prone to overeating.

Chapters Eight and Nine will discuss some of the dancers' favorite forms of exercise, but right now let's concentrate on the importance of bringing at least one half-hour of activity into your daily routine.

Remember: More than counting calories, fasting diets, steam baths or hypnosis, *increasing your physical activity is an essential part of your diet.*

- Exercise burns calories faster.

- Exercise gives you *more* energy, not less.

- Exercise keeps you younger longer.

- Exercise cuts your appetite.

- Exercise improves your stamina, your cardiovascular fitness and your overall health.

CHAPTER FOUR
A Diet to Live By

The last chapter examined the three essential rules of the Dancers' Diet:

Rule Number One: Keep your food intake to a healthy minimum.

Rule Number Two: Eat a well-rounded, balanced variety of foods.

Rule Number Three: Make exercise and physical activity a part of your diet.

In discussing these three rules, the dancers explained how important they were to their diet regimens. In *this* chapter, we'll look at a variety of structured diets you can devise in order to lose weight and keep it off for good. Before we discuss menus, however, it may be useful to discuss ways you can make sure your diet will work for you.

A Few Words About Dieting Difficulties

There seem to be dozens of reasons why the average person has a hard time sticking to a weight-loss diet. Doctors say that some of the reasons have to do with your body's metabolism and how it makes natural adjustments to offset decreased calorie intake and loss of stored fat. There is not complete agreement on how and why an individual's metabolism changes, but all agree that the changes affect the ease with which you can lose weight.

Behavioral researchers also have explored the reasons why the desire to lose weight doesn't always provide enough motivation to do so. Do we associate food and eating with love and security? Are we basically afraid of success? Are we punishing ourselves for sins we imagine we've committed? Do we simply enjoy the act of eating?

Whatever the subconscious reasons, often well hidden and confused, they can serve to sabotage our conscious self's desire to stick to a diet.

Dancers certainly aren't scientists, but they've shown themselves to be experts at losing weight! As Isabel Brown says, "I think dieting is the number-one thing on everybody's mind.

"Everybody has what is called a normal weight for her body. You can never go below that comfortably or easily, but most dancers *have* to go below that weight. In order to maintain that weight they go through incredible frustration, starving all day for one meal or being constantly on a guilt trip any time they put something in their mouths. They wake up feeling sad if they had a big meal the night before and they act sad all day.

"You have to be able to diet very slowly, not strenuously, but very slowly over a period of time. You have to be consistent and you have to know that you are taking in so many calories a day and then be able to maintain that without going crazy. It's really hard."

With that, Isabel has hit upon all of the problems a dieter, especially a dancer-dieter, faces when it comes time to lose weight.

First: If you want to become thin, you've usually got to lose weight below a level that your body feels naturally comfortable with. Struggling to deny your body what it thinks you owe it, a chocolate eclair or a sirloin steak, makes your diet a test of wills between your chubby body and your slender spirit.

Second: If eating something makes you feel guilty and sad, you've already lost the mental battle of the diet. Does the following scene sound familiar?

You're feeling a little depressed so you indulge yourself in a snack. After finishing off the potato-chip bag, you begin to feel guilty and that depresses you even more. "What's the use of dieting?" you moan, and proceed to clean out the refrigerator.

If I could design a miracle diet, I'd call it the Be Happy With Yourself Instant Weight Loss Diet.

Third: Isabel also mentions the importance of dieting slowly and consistently. Human nature being what it is, nobody wants to hear that losing ten pounds takes a long time. Everybody knows it deep down inside, but that doesn't prevent anyone from picking up a copy of the *Sassafras and Wheat Germ, Three-Day, Ten-Pound Wonder Diet* at the corner bookstore.

Fourth: And finally, there is the problem of sticking to a low-calorie diet for an extended time without losing your marbles. Learning not to indulge yourself with food at every turn, whether it's ice cream to celebrate or snack crackers to pass the time, and learning to make do with less food in the course of a day, are the surest ways to be a successful dieter—but they are also the lessons that are hardest to learn.

For most dancers the following rules, hints and tips work in overcoming these dieting difficulties:

> · Don't attempt to fight yourself over foods you don't want to eat, like cottage cheese, or over foods you feel you have to deny yourself, like sweets or breads. You won't stick to a diet that requires you to eat large quantities of a food you dislike, and if you find you're always longing for the taste of chocolate, it won't be long before you succumb to a large piece of chocolate cake. It

would be much better if you would budget yourself enough calories to indulge in a small piece of cake or candy, and you'll find you can stick to your diet if you're not feeling so sad and deprived.

· Don't try to go it alone if you're having difficulty sticking to a diet. Working with people who have similar goals is always an effective spur to dancers, and healthy, reasonable eating habits are not hard to acquire if other people are following them as well.

When Dierdre Carberry first joined ABT, one of the company's leading stars took her under her wing, rooming with her on tour and giving a little advice. "Cynthia Gregory and I are always watching what the other one is eating and we check up on each other. It's nice for someone to do that. She is a good friend, very helpful and kind . . . and a beautiful ballerina."

Mel Tomlinson also feels the beneficial influence of fellow dancers. "Being around so many healthy people rubs off on you. And then when you look at other people who seem healthy but really aren't . . . well, you know, it's your own personal choice." He goes on to describe a typical schedule when dancing with the Alvin Ailey Company, a schedule that he found most helpful in keeping weight off. "Rehearsals would start around twelve or one o'clock in the afternoon. So you could have the whole morning to eat brunch, and you would be fine for the whole day. As a part of a group, you tend to sway with the rest of the group. It's just natural."

Many people will need that kind of companionship when setting out to lose weight. Making a "contract" with a friend can give just enough motivation to get you started.

· Be patient about your weight loss. Studies show that ten pounds taken off over the course of, say, ten months are more apt to stay off than if the same ten

Mel Tomlinson of NYCB in *Agon* by George Balanchine. *(Photo copyright by Steven Caras)*

pounds are taken off in just one month's time. A long-term diet is easier to stick to, also, because its requirements are less stringent. And changing your eating habits over the long haul usually means that you've reformed your habits for good.

· Once you've successfully altered your eating habits, you'll find you have a smaller appetite. Several dancers say that the best thing about a successful diet is finding out they can get by very easily on a much smaller amount of food.

· Finally, always tailor your weight-loss diet to your own habits, your own likes and dislikes, your own schedule, and your own strengths and weaknesses.

Building Your Own Diet

The foods most dancers recommend for weight-loss and maintenance diets are fruits, eggs, chicken, fish, seafood, Chinese food, green salads, yogurt, coffee and tea, whole-wheat breads and pasta.

That's a pretty well balanced list of foods. Protein is provided by the eggs, chicken and fish, vitamins and fiber are found in fruit and green salads, yogurt has the calcium you need, and you get carbohydrates in bread and pasta. Coffee and tea are for us caffeine fiends.

Most dancers, unlike many athletes, seem to stay away from red meats, which contain large amounts of important proteins but are more fattening than chicken, eggs and fish. High on the list of dancers' no-no's is junk food: everything from packaged snacks to the all-American hamburger.

What dancers look for in a diet meal is something nutritious and satisfying, but not filling or fattening. "One thing I frequently have the urge for is an egg," says Merrill Ashley. "Eggs scrambled or in an omelet. Because, somehow, it never feels heavy and yet I can feel satisfied and not hungry. I know you shouldn't eat eggs every day, so I'll sometimes have soup instead. On the day of a performance, though, soup means too much liquid. I'll only have a bowl of soup if I can eat it early enough so that it doesn't cause me problems during a performance."

"I love seafood," says Mel Tomlinson. "I'll eat seafood any time of the day or night. It's not very high in calories, either. I love Chinese food too, because you can eat it all and feel full, but it's very low in calories."

With these suggestions in mind, here is a range of menus to lose by. The portions are small, but the nutrition is all there— two of the important rules of the Dancers' Diet—and the menus represent a variety of tastes and textures.

Please note: In most cases, young women who are still growing—and especially young ballet dancers—need more than twelve hundred calories a day, even when weight watching. If you are still growing, consult your doctor before starting this or any low-calorie diet.

The following is a week's worth of twelve-hundred-calorie days. They're menus that are balanced nutritionally, so that you're getting a selection from all four food groups: milk and cheese; protein (meat, poultry, fish, eggs, even peanut butter); vegetables and fruits; and grain (cereal, bread, rice, pasta).

Also given are approximate calorie counts for everything, but take note of the fact that they are only approximate. Calories depend on serving sizes, amounts of fat, different manufacturers, etc. Many products are sold these days with charts on the labels telling how many calories are in one serving of that specific food item, so be sure to start reading labels. You should also check packages to make sure no one is slipping hidden sugars past you (by calling them sucrose, glucose, maltose, dextrose, lactose, fructose, syrup or any other sweetener).

These calorie-counted menus do not mean that you must count calories in order to lose weight. You may follow these seven menus strictly if that helps, or you may use them as a guide to formulating your own diet regimen, made up of foods you enjoy eating and combinations you prefer.

DAY ONE

Approximate Calories

Breakfast:

1 slice whole-wheat toast	60
1 teaspoon soft margarine	35
¼ cantaloupe	40
black coffee	2

Lunch:

shrimp salad on whole-wheat bread	
¼ cup drained, canned shrimp	65
1 stalk celery, chopped	5
1 tablespoon Miracle Whip *	70
2 lettuce leaves	4
2 slices whole-wheat bread	120
black coffee or diet soda	2
	or fewer

Late Afternoon Snack:

1 fresh peach	35
½ cup plain yogurt	65

---

* Miracle Whip has about 25 fewer calories than mayonnaise in 1 tablespoon.

Dinner:

poached chicken and rice
½ chicken breast, no skin, poached in water 140
1 cup cooked white rice * 182
4 ounces sliced zucchini 19
sautéed in ½ tablespoon oil, garlic, herbs 63
4 ounces Chablis 84

Dessert, or Late Night Snack:
2½-inch slice Angel Food Cake † 135
8 ounces skim milk 80

Total Calories 1,206

DAY TWO

Approximate Calories

Breakfast:
½ cup Raisin Bran cereal 101
1 cup skim milk 80
black coffee 2

Lunch:
chicken salad on whole-wheat bread
3 ounces cooked chicken, no skin 115
2 tablespoons sour cream 50
½ medium apple, chopped 35
1 small celery stalk, chopped 4
2 slices whole-wheat bread 120
black coffee or diet soda 2
or fewer

* White rice has about 20 fewer calories than brown in 1 cup.
† See page 121 for Angel Food Cake recipe.

Late Afternoon Snack:

½ cantaloupe	80

Dinner:

4-ounce fillet of fresh flounder, broiled	130
2 teaspoons soft margarine	70
1 tablespoon lemon juice and herbs	4
3 stalks fresh broccoli, steamed	25
1 medium baked potato, no skin	90
2 tablespoons sour cream and chives	57
4 ounces Chablis	84

Late Night Snack:

2 cups popcorn, salted, no butter	108

Total Calories	1,157

DAY THREE

Approximate Calories

Breakfast:

toasted bagel	165
1 tablespoon whipped cream cheese *	36
black coffee	2

Lunch:

¼ head lettuce	15
large, hard-boiled egg	80
5 green olives	30

* Whipped cream cheese has about ⅓ the calories of solid cream cheese.

1 raw carrot, cut in sticks	20
1 tablespoon French dressing	60
black coffee or diet soda	2
	or fewer

Late Afternoon Snack:

1 medium apple	70
1-ounce stick of cheddar cheese	113

Dinner:

½ cup spaghetti, cooked 14–20 minutes	78
4 ounces marinara sauce	70
1 tablespoon grated cheese	27
1 medium tomato, sliced	33
½ medium cucumber, peeled and sliced	15
1 tablespoon vinegar and herbs	3
2 plain bread sticks	80
4 ounces Chianti	88

Dessert, or Late Night Snack:

1 small orange	65
10 large strawberries	37
½ cup low-fat cottage cheese	77

Total Calories	1,166

DAY FOUR

Approximate Calories

Breakfast:

1 slice whole-wheat toast	60
1 teaspoon soft margarine	35

½ grapefruit	41
black coffee	2

Lunch:

1 cup strawberry yogurt	260
black coffee or diet soda	2
	or fewer

Late Afternoon Snack:

6 ounces apple juice	85
1 raw carrot, cut in sticks	20

Dinner:

cheese omelet	
2 large eggs, herbs, salt and pepper	160
⅓ cup shredded cheddar cheese	113
½ tablespoon soft margarine	50
1 tablespoon half-and-half cream	19
2 plain bread sticks	80
½ head Boston lettuce	15
1 medium tomato, in wedges	33
1 tablespoon Italian dressing	90
4 ounces Chablis	84

Late Night Snack:

1 cup popcorn, salted, no butter	54

Total Calories	1,203

DAY FIVE

Approximate Calories

Breakfast:
½ cup All-Bran cereal	100
1 cup skim milk	80
½ cup sliced banana	64
black coffee	2

Lunch:
peanut butter and jelly sandwich	
2 tablespoons peanut butter	184
1 tablespoon grape jelly	50
2 slices whole-wheat bread	120
black coffee or diet soda	2
	or fewer

Late Afternoon Snack:
1 fresh peach	35
½ cup plain yogurt	65

Dinner:
3-ounce lamb chop, broiled, no fat	160
1 cup cooked white rice	182
10 mushrooms, sliced	28
½ cup green beans, steamed	15
4 ounces Beaujolais	80

Dessert, or Late Night Snack
½ cantaloupe	80

Total Calories   1,247

DAY SIX

Approximate Calories

Breakfast:
6 ounces tomato juice	35
1 large egg, soft-boiled	80
1 teaspoon soft margarine	35
1 slice whole-wheat toast	60
black coffee	2

Lunch:
1 cup blueberry yogurt	260
black coffee or diet soda	2
	or fewer

Late Afternoon Snack:
1 chocolate-nut brownie	54
6 ounces apple juice	85

Dinner:
Chinese food
1 cup cooked white rice	182
2 shrimp egg rolls	128
1 cup chicken chow mein	74
Chinese tea, no sugar	1

Dessert, or Late Night Snack:
1 small orange	65
½ cup low-fat cottage cheese	77

Total Calories 1,140

Day Seven

Approximate Calories

Breakfast:
½ grapefruit   41
1 honey-bran muffin   154
black coffee   2

Lunch:
tuna salad on whole-wheat bread
3½ ounces tuna, water-packed   108
1 stalk celery, chopped   5
2 small green onions, chopped   7
1 tablespoon Miracle Whip   70
2 slices whole-wheat bread   120
black coffee or diet soda   2
                                                           or fewer

Late Afternoon Snack:
1 cup beef barley soup   83

Dinner:
crab-meat salad
3½ ounces fresh, cooked crab meat   93
1 large egg, hard-boiled   80
½ head Boston lettuce   15
1 medium tomato, in wedges   33
1 tablespoon Russian dressing   58
5 saltine crackers   60
4 ounces Chablis   84

Dessert, or Late Night Snack:
½ cup orange sherbet   120

Total Calories   1,135

In looking over the previous seven menus, you may have no-ticed the absence of a few foods. Most noticeably, nearly all red meats have been omitted from the diet menus. Dancers recom-mend keeping meat to a minimum, but a dieter must make cer-tain to replace hamburgers, steaks, and pork chops with plenty of chicken, fish, eggs and peanut butter in order to get enough protein for an active lifestyle. (Also absent are peas and beans, which are too gassy and obviously not recommended for dancers' diets!)

The menus, while keeping to a general maximum of about twelve hundred calories a day, do not totally restrict the con-sumption of fats and sugars, which are important elements of a balanced diet. Using small amounts of margarine, salad dress-ings, mayonnaise and vegetable oils keeps calories down but pro-vides the necessary fat in your diet. Also included in the menus are one or two sweet treats, namely the Angel Food Cake, the chocolate-nut brownie and the orange sherbet. Making sure, of course, that the portions are small ones, you shouldn't feel hesi-tant about rewarding yourself with these or similar treats. They'll help you avoid feeling deprived of or starved for something spe-cial. They also provide a little shot of sugar, which many dancers find essential for extra energy.

There are servings of wine with all but one of the dinners in our twelve-hundred-calorie-a-day menus. A four-ounce serving of most fine wines, with the exception of a few sweet wines like Sauternes, port and sherry, will set you back no more than 100 calories. One jigger (1½ ounce) of most distilled spirits, such as gin, vodka, rum and whiskey, will run in the neighborhood of 100 to 125 calories. Beer and ale are also relatively fattening beverages. A 12-ounce can of beer contains 150 or more calories; new "lite" brands contain far fewer.

One final recommendation is that you drink. Besides flushing your system of impurities, a large intake of fluids can help you avoid feeling empty during a diet. Water, carbonated water, iced tea (with lemon but without sugar), black coffee, hot tea and diet sodas are minimum-calorie beverages. Another alternative to keep in mind is the six-calorie beef-bouillon break!

A Maintenance Diet

The trouble with every diet is that once you've successfully taken off the ten, twenty or more pounds you had planned to take off, you also lose the motivation to watch what you're eating and to keep at your exercise regimen.

Maybe you celebrate your weight loss with a five-course meal, or all the ice cream you can eat. Maybe you find that it's too cold to walk today, or that you're running late for your exercise class. So what's the harm of that? After all, the weight has been lost and there's no need to worry about sticking to all those good habits you worked so hard to acquire, right?

Of course that couldn't be more wrong.

The point of losing weight and becoming more active in the first place was not to reach your ideal weight for a day or a week or even a month. It was to become slender, active and healthy *for the rest of your life.* Why did you work so hard to lose those pounds if, having lost them, you promptly gain them right back?

Once the motivation to *lose* weight is gone, don't replace it with the old careless attitudes toward eating and exercise. You must be just as anxious to take in only as many calories as you expend to maintain that ideal weight as you were to eat fewer calories while raising your calorie expenditure when you wanted to lose pounds.

For that reason, the next seven menus can help you budget your calories, just as you did when losing weight, in order to maintain the weight that's right for you. At sixteen hundred calories a day you'll find that pounds will not creep up on you and that the figure you worked so hard for will continue to be the figure you see in the mirror every morning.

The maintenance plan works the same way as the weight-loss plan does. While calorie counting is not essential, it's a good way to keep track of what you eat. The primary rule is to use the following menus as a guide to portions, nutritional balance and relative caloric values.

Once again, a vital element of these maintenance-diet menus is strict adherence to thirty minutes of challenging physical activity every day. Faithfully following that regimen makes every diet, weight-loss and maintenance, that much more effective.

Be flexible about your diet to live by. If you eat too heavily one day, cut back on your next day's meals. If you absolutely, positively can't get your thirty minutes of exercise, restrict your diet to twelve hundred to fourteen hundred calories. Or, to pay for the extra helping of spaghetti, increase your thirty minutes of exercise to forty-five or sixty minutes.

With these menus, or those you develop yourself, you can get off the dieting seesaw that found you gaining back two pounds for every one you'd lost. A diet to live by means just that— staying slender and healthy as a way of life. Dancers say it's the only way to be!

MAINTENANCE DIET—DAY ONE

Approximate Calories

Breakfast:

large, poached egg	80
1 honey-bran muffin	154
1 teaspoon soft margarine	35
½ grapefruit	41
coffee with 1 tablespoon half-and-half cream	21

Lunch:

1 cup chicken-noodle soup	75
green salad	
½ head Boston lettuce	15
1 medium tomato	33
⅓ cup shredded cheddar cheese	113
1 tablespoon Italian dressing	90
1 chocolate-nut brownie	54
diet soda	2
	or fewer

Late Afternoon Snack:

½ cantaloupe	80
coffee with 1 tablespoon half-and-half cream	21

Dinner:

Shrimp Creole with rice *	
¼ pound shrimp, peeled and deveined	103
medium green pepper, chopped	15

* See recipe for Shrimp Creole, page 111.

medium onion, chopped	40
small stalk of celery, chopped	4
2 whole, canned tomatoes, crushed	28
sautéed in 1 teaspoon margarine, thyme,	
bay leaf, crushed garlic clove and salt and	
pepper	35
1 cup cooked white rice	182
1 small dinner roll	85
1 teaspoon soft margarine	35
4 ounces Beaujolais	80

Late Night Snack:

2 cups popcorn, salted, no butter	108

Total Calories	1,529

MAINTENANCE DIET—DAY TWO

Approximate Calories

Breakfast:

¾ cup oatmeal	100
½ tablespoon honey	32
1 tablespoon half-and-half cream	19
½ cantaloupe	80
black coffee	2

Lunch:

ham and cheese sandwich	
4 ounces sliced ham	123
1 ounce Swiss cheese	104
1 tablespoon Miracle Whip	70
2 slices whole-wheat bread	120
diet soda	2
	or fewer

Late Afternoon Snack:

1 fresh peach	35
½ cup low-fat cottage cheese	77

Dinner:

1 whole chicken breast, no skin	280
sauteed in wine, chicken broth and herbs	30
¾ cup cooked noodles	150
1 teaspoon soft margarine	35
1 tablespoon grated cheese	27
4 ounces sliced zucchini	19
1 medium tomato, chopped	33
sautéed in ½ tablespoon oil, garlic, herbs	63
4 ounces Chablis	84

Late Night Snack:

½ cup orange sherbet	120

Total Calories	1,605

MAINTENANCE DIET—DAY THREE

Approximate Calories

Breakfast:

large, scrambled egg	80
1 tablespoon half-and-half cream	19
2 teaspoons soft margarine	70
1 slice whole-wheat toast	60
½ cup orange juice	60
coffee with 1 tablespoon half-and-half cream	21

Lunch:

shrimp salad on whole-wheat bread *	264
diet soda	2
	or fewer

Late Afternoon Snack:

1 cup cherry yogurt	270
coffee with half-and-half cream	21

Dinner:

½ cup spaghetti, cooked 14–20 minutes	78
4 ounces marinara sauce	70
1 tablespoon grated cheese	27
½ head Boston lettuce	15
1 medium tomato, sliced	33
½ medium cucumber, chopped	15
1 tablespoon Italian dressing	90
2 plain bread sticks	80
4 ounces Chianti	88

Dessert, or Late Night Snack:

1 square banana-walnut cake	205

Total Calories	1,568

* See page 82 for ingredients of shrimp-salad sandwich.

Maintenance Diet—Day Four

Approximate Calories

Breakfast:
2-egg cheese omelet *	342
coffee with 1 tablespoon half-and-half cream	21

Lunch:

chef salad
½ head Boston lettuce	15
1 medium tomato, sliced	33
½ cup sliced cheddar cheese	169
2 ounces sliced ham	62
1 green pepper, sliced	15
2 tablespoons French dressing	120
diet soda	2
	or fewer

Snack:
½ cantaloupe	80
1 cup skim milk	80

Dinner:

Veal Goulash †
3 ounces veal, cut in 2-inch cubes	230
½ medium onion, sliced	20

* See page 86 for ingredients of cheese omelet.
† See Chapter Five for Veal Goulash recipe.

beef broth, tomato paste, paprika, vinegar and caraway seeds	50
2 tablespoons sour cream	57
1 small dinner roll	85
1 teaspoon soft margarine	35
½ cup steamed green beans	15
4 ounces Beaujolais	80

Late Night Snack:

2 cups popcorn, salted, no butter	108

Total Calories	1,619

MAINTENANCE DIET—DAY FIVE

Approximate Calories

Breakfast:

½ grapefruit	41
½ cup Raisin Bran cereal	101
1 cup skim milk	80
coffee with 1 tablespoon half-and-half-cream	21

Lunch:

1-cup serving of chili con carne	450
1 corn muffin	140
1 teaspoon soft margarine	35
diet soda	2 or fewer

Late Afternoon Snack:

1 medium apple	70

Dinner:
3 ounces broiled salmon, with dill and lemon
    juice   155
½ ounce scalloped potatoes   150
3 stalks steamed broccoli   25
1 teaspoon soft margarine   35
2 bread sticks   80
4 ounces Chablis   80

Dessert, or Late Night Snack:
2½-inch slice Angel Food Cake *   135

Total Calories   1,600

MAINTENANCE DIET—DAY SIX

Approximate Calories

Breakfast:
toasted bagel   165
1 tablespoon whipped cream cheese   36
coffee with 1 tablespoon half-and-half cream   21

Lunch:
1 cup Manhattan clam chowder   75
1 slice whole-wheat toast   60
1 teaspoon soft margarine   35
diet soda   2
    or fewer

* See page 121 for Angel Food Cake recipe.

Late Afternoon Snack:
1 medium tangerine	40
½ cup plain yogurt	65

Dinner:
6-ounce sirloin steak, broiled	660
1 medium potato, baked, no skin	90
2 tablespoons sour cream and chives	57
6 asparagus spears, steamed	20
¼ cup hollandaise sauce	75
4 ounces Beaujolais	80

Late Night Snack:
2 cups popcorn, salted, no butter	108

Total Calories	1,589

MAINTENANCE DIET—DAY SEVEN

Approximate Calories

Breakfast:
large egg, poached	80
1 honey-bran muffin	154
1 teaspoon soft margarine	35
coffee with 1 tablespoon half-and-half cream	21

Lunch:
tuna salad on whole-wheat bread *	310
diet soda	2
	or fewer

* See page 89 for ingredients of tuna-salad sandwich.

Late Afternoon Snack:
1 cup raspberry yogurt	278
coffee with half-and-half cream	21

Dinner:
3 chicken drumsticks, fried	270
½ cup mashed potatoes	130
¼ cup light chicken gravy *	25
1 ear sweet corn-on-the-cob, boiled	70
1 tablespoon soft margarine	105
4 ounces Chablis	84

Dessert, or Late Night Snack:
¼ cantaloupe	40

Total Calories	1,625

To sum up the rules of a Diet to Live By:

· Keep calories low, nutrition balanced and foods varied.

· Tailor your diet menus to your own likes and dislikes, to your own schedule and to a regimen that you can follow and even enjoy.

· Always try to substitute low-calorie foods for high-calorie ones. For example: half a chicken breast (140 calories) for a hamburger and roll (280 calories); one tablespoon of sour cream (28 calories) for one of butter

---

*Chicken gravy, prepared from a mix, can contain anywhere from 20 to 85 calories per ¼ cup, so check the label. If you make it from scratch, skim all the fat you can, and rely on herbs and spices for flavor instead of fats, to keep calories as low as possible.

(100 calories); or a medium baked potato without the skin (90 calories) for a serving of instant mashed potatoes (130 calories).

- Don't snack unless you've budgeted for those calories.

- Don't go overboard when you're going out to eat. Make adjustments for larger meals by cutting down on the rest of your daily menu.

- Most important: *Check with a doctor before you go on any diet!*

CHAPTER FIVE

Food for Dance: Dancers' Recipes— Low-Calorie and Otherwise

Some dancers hate to cook. Some dancers wouldn't know a spatula from a Cuisinart. Most dancers simply don't have the time to prepare a meal unless it's out of a can.

I sometimes enjoy being creative in the kitchen, until my daughter begs me, "Please, Mommy, make something *normal!*"

But there are dancers who are not only good cooks, they also enjoy the recreation of preparing fine food and sitting down to a home-cooked meal with friends.

Some of the following recipes, offered by the dancers themselves, are low-calorie treasures—nutritious and tasty. A couple of them are examples of that dancers' vice known as "the pigout," when calories don't count and tomorrow will never come!

Before you get out the pots and pans, however, take a look at these pointers on cooking with a minimum of calories:

- Cook without oil: Use non-stick pans; broil meats instead of browning them in fat; poach and braise meats and fish (cooking in liquid) instead of sautéing in fat; spray pans with nonstick products.

- Get into the habit of removing fat from foods: Trim cuts of meat and poultry *before* cooking; chill soups and remove the solidified fat; remove fat from any refrigerated leftover before reheating.

ABT's Gelsey Kirkland wearing a babushka and keeping warm at the barre. (*Photo copyright by Steven Caras*)

- Substitute low-calorie staples for high-calorie meats: In soups, stews and casseroles, substitute rice, noodles, vegetables, grains, etc., for portions of meat; in meat-based salads, substitute crunchy raw vegetables.

- Choose fish or poultry over beef, pork or lamb.

- Be lavish with seasonings other than salt and butter: Learn to use fresh herbs; add lemon or lime juice; canned broths are a good flavor substitute; other flavorful substitutes are vinegar, Tabasco sauce, onions, garlic, Worcestershire sauce, etc.

- In recipes that call for sliced meats, slice meats very thin—small amounts of meat seem to go farther.

- Always cook with skim or low-fat milk.

FAST GAZPACHO

4 large tomatoes
2 green peppers
1 large cucumber, peeled
1 small onion, peeled
1 garlic clove, chopped
   (or a pinch of garlic
   powder,
   if you prefer)

1 can of beef bouillon
juice of ½ lemon
2 tablespoons vegetable oil
salt and pepper
dash of Tabasco

Cut all the vegetables into one- to two-inch chunks. Stick them in the blender or food processor, along with the garlic, the bouillon, the lemon juice and the oil.

Process or blenderize the mixture to a puree. Pour into a container (glass or plastic), cover and chill.

When the soup has reached a cold enough temperature, taste it and season it with salt, pepper and dash of Tabasco.

This soup serves about five people. It should be eaten quite cold, with a selection of crunchy garnishes: croutons, chopped green onion, chopped cucumber, chopped parsley, chopped green pepper, and the like.

The beauty of this soup is that it is fast and easy to prepare, spicy and refreshing, and under one hundred calories a serving!

ISABEL BROWN'S CRUNCHY SALAD

Isabel says, "This is crunchy and not too fattening—provided you don't use too much salad dressing."

½ head of red cabbage, sliced
1 large tomato
1 carrot, cut up
a few raw string beans
a few slices of red onion

a few Chinese pea pods ("If you can afford them," Isabel adds.)
¼ cup sunflower seeds
1 small can of white, solid tuna fish in water

Toss all ingredients together in a bowl. This is enough to serve one person.

"I make my own salad dressing, one quart of it to start with—it lasts for a while," says Isabel.

Salad Dressing

Fill one fourth of a one-quart jar with olive oil, one fourth with salad oil, and fill the rest of the jar with wine vinegar. Add two tablespoons of brown sugar, two tablespoons of salt, one tablespoon of pepper and one and a half tablespoons of Salad Supreme to the jar. Shake it all up, and serve.

JACQUES D'AMBOISE'S WONDERFUL DINNER SALAD

"First of all the dressing: lots of dried mustard, about a table-spoon; three tablespoons of vinegar, preferably a red wine vine-gar; and one or two tablespoons of soy sauce (I use that instead of salt); and then about three tablespoons of olive oil. (You can use olive oil, or a polyunsaturated oil like soy bean—but I like the taste of olive oil. Switch olive oils every once in a while—use a Spanish, which is kind of strong, or a Greek—because the oil has its own individual taste.)

"Now buy Alfonso olives and add them, and chop raw red onion, or the white part of scallions, and add them to the dress-ing or to the salad. Again, this is all according to taste, whether you want to go heavy or strong on the onions, but what you have is a very tangy kind of dressing.

"Now, with the combination of spicy dressing and salad, this is a dinner. First, vegetables: I slice celery lengthwise so that they make long slivers, and add good Greek olives (I'm crazy about them, I love olives). Don't get the usual delicatessen olive, go to a Greek store and get them.

"Now what I like to do is take one big slice of Genoa salami, or any kind of really spicy salami, and you chop it into little tiny cubes. Add that to your dressing, and one other thing (I like it, but you could leave it out) is a very bland cheese, also diced, like a Jack or other fairly hard cheese. I like the combination of cheese and spicy salami and the tangy dressing with the olives I love. (I'll eat anything accompanied by an olive.)"

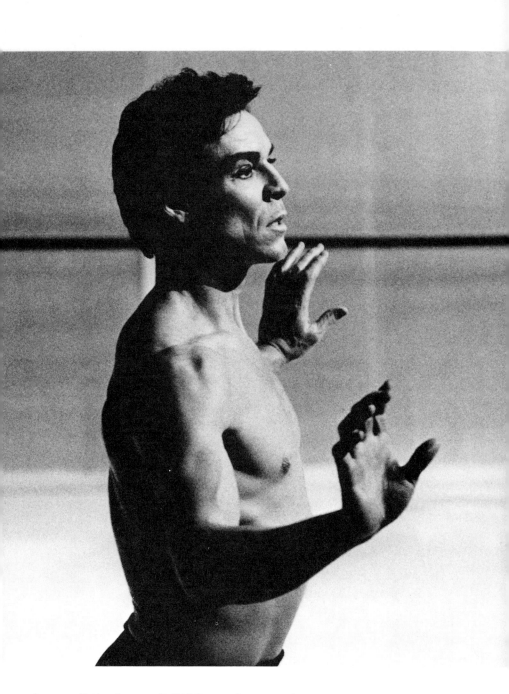

Jacques D'Amboise of NYCB in *Afternoon of a Faun* by Jerome
Robbins. *(Photo copyright by Steven Caras)*

DIET PICKER-UPPERS

These sauces can make dull fish fillets and boring chicken breasts snappy, when dieting menus start to get you down.

Lemon 'n' Egg Sauce

¼ cup of flour
2 cups of skim milk
salt and pepper

1 tablespoon fresh lemon
  juice
2 hard-boiled eggs
a few sprigs of fresh dill

Heating the flour, skim milk and salt and pepper to taste in a nonstick pan over medium heat, make a smooth, thick white sauce while stirring constantly. Just before serving, add the lemon juice and eggs, which have been chopped, to the pan. Continue to cook the sauce until it is heated through. Garnish with the dill. This makes a little more than two cups of sauce, and is delicious served over fish or vegetables.

All-purpose Curry Sauce

1 6-ounce can of tomato
  paste
2 cups unsweetened apple
  juice
1 teaspoon curry powder

⅛ teaspoon ground cumin
½ teaspoon poultry
  seasoning
¼ cup raisins

Heat all the ingredients in a saucepan over medium-high heat until thick. Curry Sauce goes well with meat, poultry, shellfish and rice, and can even perk up leftovers.

INDIAN-STYLE ROAST CHICKEN

1 broiler chicken	1 tablespoon coriander
1 cup plain, low-fat yogurt	1 tablespoon turmeric
2 cloves of garlic, crushed	2 teaspoons cumin
1 tablespoon ginger	1 tablespoon cayenne pepper
juice of ½ lemon	sliced lemons and onions

Wash and dry the chicken, and remove visible traces of fat. Mix the yogurt, lemon juice, garlic and seasonings together, and then rub the mixture over the chicken, inside and out. Wrap, and refrigerate the marinated chicken for a day, turning it over once or twice.

Put the chicken into a roasting pan and roast in a 425° oven for about one hour. Baste frequently. Check at the end of an hour if the leg-joint juices run clear, or if the interior joint registers 160° F. The chicken should be a lovely brown.

Serve the pieces of chicken with the sliced lemons and onions. The chicken can be eaten with or without the skin (without the skin means fewer calories per serving.)

SHRIMP CREOLE

1 pound fresh shrimp, peeled and deveined	1 can whole, peeled tomatoes
1½ tablespoons margarine	pinch of thyme
3 medium green peppers, cut in chunks	2 bay leaves
3 medium onions, chopped	2 garlic cloves, crushed
2 stalks of celery, chopped	salt, pepper, hot sauce to taste

After peeling and cleaning the shrimp, sauté them in the margarine in a large nonstick skillet for ten minutes. Add the peppers, onions and celery and continue to sauté until the vegetables are just tender, about ten minutes.

Crush the canned tomatoes, and add them to the skillet, juice and all. Stir in the seasonings and garlic, and cook for ten minutes more. Don't add much hot sauce at first—just a little for its zing.

Makes 4 servings.

MARTINE VAN HAMEL'S "PUTTING THE RICE TO BED"

Martine's grandmother and mother made rice this unusual way.

White Rice	*Brown Rice*
3 cups of rice	1 cup of rice
5 cups of water	2 cups of water

Bring the rice to a boil, then lower heat to a simmer and stir once. Cook for about ten minutes, or until no water is visible. Do not stir.

Put a good tight lid on the pot, and "put it to bed"!

You can wrap pillows, quilts, newspapers or anything around the pot to insulate it, leave the whole thing in a corner somewhere and forget it for hours.

Martine wraps hers in blankets and pillows and leaves it on the bed until dinner time.

"This is an old Canadian recipe," Martine adds. "My grandmother never measured the rice and water—she would use her finger to get the right amounts!"

Martine Van Hamel of ABT "putting the rice to bed." (*Photo copyright © 1983 by James J. Camner*)

SUZANNE FARRELL'S COLD SALMON WITH WATERCRESS MOUSSELINE

4 fresh salmon steaks	1 bay leaf
2½ cups of water	juice of 1 lemon
½ large onion, sliced	salt and freshly ground
1 or 2 stalks of celery, sliced	pepper

Combine water, sliced onion, celery, bay leaf, lemon juice, and salt and pepper to taste in a wide saucepan. Bring to a boil, then reduce the heat and simmer gently for fifteen minutes.

Add salmon steaks to the simmering liquid, carefully placing them in the pan without overlap. Cover the pan and simmer for ten minutes, or until fish flakes easily with a fork.

Chill the steaks in their own liquid. Just before serving, drain. Serve with the mousseline. Serves four.

Watercress Mousseline

2 bunches of watercress	salt and freshly ground
⅔ cup heavy cream	pepper

Remove leaves from watercress; place them in cold water. Bring to a boil and let simmer for ten minutes. Rinse well in cold water. Drain and pass through a fine sieve.

Bring heavy cream to a boil in a saucepan. Add sieved watercress and season to taste with salt and pepper. *Chill.*

Just before serving, whisk until thick and smooth.

A note from Suzanne: "Easy to prepare and takes very little time!"

Suzanne Farrell with Jorge Donn in Maurice Béjart's productions of
Nijinsky. (Photo copyright by W. Reilly)

AUSTRIAN-STYLE VEAL GOULASH

1 pound veal stew meat
2 medium onions, sliced thin
salt to taste
1 tablespoon paprika
¼ cup sour cream

1 can beef broth
1 tablespoon tomato paste
1 tablespoon wine vinegar
1 teaspoon caraway seed

Trim the veal of all fat and cut it into two-inch cubes. Instead of browning the meat in fat, place the veal cubes on a broiler pan and place under the broiler for several minutes, just until browned. Pour the meat juices from the broiler pan into a large Dutch oven or soup kettle; heat on top of the stove. Add the onion slices to the meat juices and cook, stirring, until golden brown. Sprinkle the paprika over the onions, stir briefly, and then add about ¼ cup of the beef broth.

Add the meat to the pan. Cook for three minutes, stirring frequently. Add the remainder of the beef broth, the tomato paste, vinegar, caraway seeds and salt. Cover the pan tightly, lower the heat, and simmer for about forty-five minutes, or until the veal is tender. Just before serving, stir in the sour cream and simmer until heated through. Makes 4 servings.

Goulash goes well with egg noodles or steamed potatoes.

STIR-FRIED CHINESE BEEF AND VEGETABLES

¾ pound round steak
¼ cup soy sauce
2 tablespoons sherry

1 tablespoon vegetable oil
1½ to 2 cups of vegetables:
   sliced green peppers,

1 tablespoon cornstarch
½ teaspoon ginger
clove of garlic, minced

Chinese pea pods, sliced
mushrooms, bamboo
shoots, sliced water
chestnuts, etc.

If the round steak is partially frozen, it is easy to slice into very thin one- to two-inch strips.

Mix the soy sauce, sherry, cornstarch, ginger and garlic in a small bowl. Heat the oil in a large frying pan or wok, add the beef and quickly stir-fry. Remove beef from pan.

Add the vegetables, already sliced and ready, and stir-fry over high heat for approximately five minutes, or until the vegetables are cooked but still crisp. Add the beef again, stir together with the vegetables, and then push the mixture to the sides of the pan. Add the soy-sauce mixture to the pan, heat to boiling, and cook for one minute. Stir sauce together with the beef and vegetables. Serve immediately. Serves four.

DARCI KISTLER'S FRUITY MILK SHAKE

1 large ripe peach, or
nectarine, peeled, pitted
and cut into large chunks;
or 4 to 5 whole
strawberries, hulled; or ½
cup fresh whole
raspberries; or 1 medium
banana, sliced

⅓ cup instant nonfat milk
powder
½ teaspoon vanilla or
almond extract
3 ice cubes
water

Place the ice cubes in a one-cup measure, and add water up to the one-cup mark. Combine the ice water and all the other ingredients in a blender, and process until the ice has completely melted.

Serve in a glass, and garnish with a strawberry or a mint leaf. Serves one.

FROZEN FRUIT GRANITA

1 10-ounce package of frozen
   strawberries or raspberries
1 teaspoon Cointreau

1 orange, both the juice and
   the grated peel

Allow the frozen berries to thaw slightly, and then cut the package into large chunks. Add the orange peel, juice and liqueur to a blender. Whir in the blender, adding chunks of berries a few at a time.

Spoon the puree into chilled serving dishes, and freeze for one and a half hours or more. Serves three to four.

MEL TOMLINSON'S PINEAPPLE DUMP CAKE

"This is called a dump cake," says Mel, "and the reason it's called a dump cake is because there is no messing and no mess. This recipe was in our family. My aunt gave it to my mother, who gave it to me, and I've passed it on to lots of other people to try. It's just the right thing when you have the munchies. Oh, it's wonderful . . . it's for the times when I just don't care about calories."

1 box of cake mix
1 stick of butter

1 can of fruit: crushed
   pineapple, or apple pie
   filling

Mel Tomlinson and Heather Watts of NYCB in *Agon*. *(Photo copyright © 1983 by Martha Swope)*

Put the fruit in the bottom of an old-fashioned iron frying pan, including the syrup. Dump the cake mix on top of the fruit. Melt the stick of butter and pour it on top of the cake mix, pouring it evenly over the surface.

Bake the cake in a 400° oven for thirty-five minutes. "It will turn a nice golden brown," Mel says, "and you just let it set on top of the stove to cool. Give it five minutes—it gives you forty minutes of waiting altogether—and the butter has caused the top of the cake to harden. It's all moist underneath with a hard crust on top—it's marvelous!"

DIERDRE CARBERRY'S FAVORITE COOKIES

Dierdre's Giant Chocolate Chips

2 cups of flour
1 teaspoon baking soda
1 teaspoon salt
1 cup butter (½ pound), softened
1½ cups of sugar
1 large egg

1½ teaspoons vanilla extract
2 teaspoons strong brewed coffee or Kahlua
1 12-ounce package of chocolate chips
1 cup chopped walnuts or pecans

Mix the flour, baking soda and salt; set aside. In a large bowl, cream the butter until fluffy and then gradually beat in the sugar until light. Beat in the egg, vanilla and coffee until well blended and fluffy. Add the flour mixture, and stir until well blended; finally stir in the chocolate and nuts.

Shape the cookies into two-inch balls and place them three inches apart on an *ungreased* cookie sheet (about six per sheet). Bake on the middle rack of a preheated 350° oven for twenty to twenty-three minutes, or until the cookies are golden and the edges lightly browned. Cool them completely on the cookie sheets. Store, covered, in a dry, cool place. This recipe makes about twenty-one four-inch cookies. Dierdre adds, "The recipe may be halved, but include one whole egg."

Dierdre's Almond Meringue Kisses

½ cup sifted cake flour
4 tablespoons granulated
  sugar
4 egg whites, room
  temperature

¼ teaspoon of salt
pinch of cream of tartar
1 teaspoon almond extract

Sift the flour with two tablespoons of sugar and set aside.

Combine the egg whites, salt and cream of tartar and beat until stiff. Gradually beat in the remaining two tablespoons of sugar, then gradually beat in the flour mixture. Fold in the almond extract, being careful not to deflate the meringue.

Line cookie sheets with aluminum foil and, using a teaspoon, "drop" the meringues onto the sheets one half-inch apart. Bake in a preheated 275° oven for forty-five minutes, or until crisp and golden brown. Remove to racks and cool, then carefully peel the cookies from the foil.

"This recipe makes seventy cookies," says Dierdre, "at approximately five and a half calories apiece."

ANGEL FOOD CAKE

1 cup cake flour, sifted
1¼ cups sugar, sifted
¼ teaspoon salt
whites of 10 large eggs or
  12 medium eggs

1 tablespoon water
1 tablespoon lemon juice
1⅓ teaspoons cream of tartar
½ teaspoon vanilla extract
½ teaspoon almond extract

Sift the cake flour first, then add to it ¼ cup of the sugar, and the salt. Sift the three ingredients together two times.

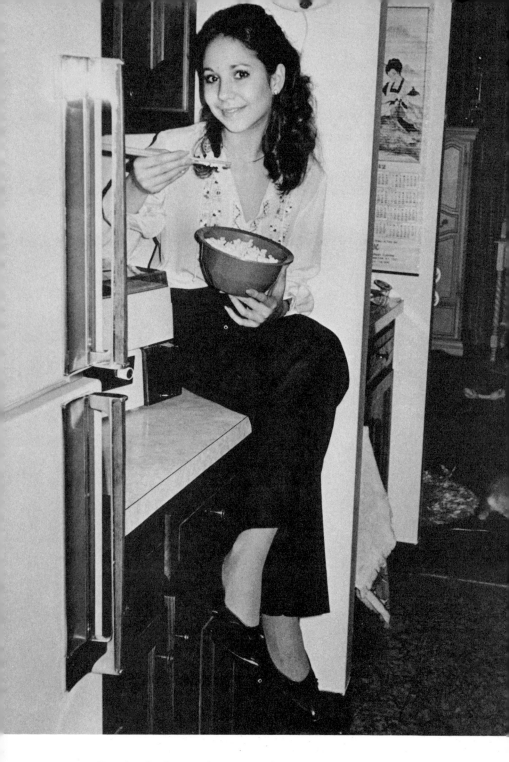

Dierdre Carberry of ABT snacks on popcorn—only fifty-four calories per cup. (*Photo copyright © 1983 by James J. Camner*)

In a large bowl, beat the egg whites with the water and lemon juice until just stiff. Beat in the cream of tartar, then gradually add the remaining cup of sugar by sprinkling it by ¼ cup measures over the egg whites and beating it in. Add the vanilla and almond flavorings and beat just to mix thoroughly.

Now carefully fold in the flour, sugar and salt mixture, using a spatula or wooden spoon to mix the ingredients without deflating the egg whites. Pour the cake batter into an ungreased tube pan, and bake for forty to fifty minutes at 350°, or until the surface is lightly browned and a toothpick inserted into the center of the cake comes out clean.

Remove the cake from the oven and invert the pan, propping it on a funnel or a bottle neck. Let the cake cool for at least an hour. Once a spatula is used to loosen the edges of the cake, it should come out of the pan cleanly and easily. As Angel Food Cake is so light and delicate, use the tines of a fork instead of a knife to cut it.

CHAPTER SIX
The Chain Around the Refrigerator

Dancers are all too familiar with the folly of fad diets—this chapter takes a look at some of the bizarre and silly diets that dancers have tried. All of them, as we've said before, ultimately ended in failure. These diets have been tried and found wanting. They are certified flops!

I've found that one of the best ways to stay on a diet is to have very little food in the house. But I also have three children, including a son who is very skinny and always hungry. Instead of keeping only low-cal foods in the kitchen, I had to learn a way to walk past the refrigerator very quickly. Every time the refrigerator door opened my willpower disappeared.

After some time spent fighting the urge to eat, I discovered that my son had a large padlock, and I persuaded him to put a chain around the refrigerator door and lock it up.

This terrific idea worked well for a while, because every time I wanted something to eat I had to go and get him to unlock it for me. It was hard to explain, though, when people came by and saw the refrigerator chained up. . . .

Because I get up before the children most mornings, the locked-up refrigerator became more and more inconvenient and more and more annoying. One day, out of sheer frustration, I sawed off the lock.

That was the end of the padlock diet.

Next I tried putting an alarm in the refrigerator, one that

would go off every time the door was opened. This soon drove everybody crazy, and so that was the end of the alarm diet.

I think it all started when I joined the New York City Ballet. Before then I ate what I wanted, even a butterscotch sundae with almonds after dance class. After joining the company, however, I noticed everyone's fear of and obsession with food. So I began to worry about it too. It was a short step from that to padlocks and refrigerator alarms.

Another fellow New York City Ballet dancer is Toni Bentley, author of *A Winter Season,* and she shares some stories of dancing and dieting. "I don't know of any dancers who haven't tried different diets. I think I went on one before I ever needed to just because it was fashionable. You know the kids in school. Everybody's dieting, so when you wake up in the morning you try and decide what you'll eat that day instead of just being natural about it."

When asked if she feels that fad diets create problems for dancers, Toni answers, "Yes, certainly. If you don't put any food in your mouth, you start feeling faint. And sometimes in a performance you get the most awful feeling and suddenly think, I didn't get enough to eat and I can't make it. . . . It's very bad. If it happens to you, try and learn about yourself so it doesn't happen again."

Another dancer who has had some experience with unusual dieting methods is Susan Jaffe. "I tried fad diets a long time ago, but I found out that they didn't work." When Susan was required to lose ten pounds before joining ABT, she went to a diet doctor. Even that, however, proved dangerously extreme.

"Well . . . I had to take vitamin B shots. I had to give myself the shots in my leg every day. I also had a diet of only five hundred calories. There were all these special recipes where you use Pam instead of oil, and certain kinds of bread. You were allowed two grapes, or one apple, or a teaspoon of milk in your coffee. There were all of those diet things to buy, like Alba 77, sugar-free jam . . . I hated every minute of it!"

Susan Jaffe and Mikhail Baryshnikov in *Other Dances* by Jerome
Robbins. *(Photo copyright © 1983 by Martha Swope)*

Susan now controls her weight by eating moderately but nutritiously and she's skeptical of the fad diets that circulate through the company. "There was a tofu [Japanese bean curd] diet, where people would eat just that to lose weight. I remember three years ago, some girls used to eat just ice cream . . . that was their diet! I think they may have actually lost weight, but I never tried things like that. They were too crazy."

Pressure from other people seems to be a major reason for weight control, and weight gain too. Peer pressure might cause young ballerinas to try silly fads, but family and friends can also make it hard for a dancer to watch what he or she eats. Mel Tomlinson has felt pressure from both sides and describes the way he was influenced by well-meaning friends.

"I had always been very thin. I could eat as much as I wanted to and I never had a problem about what I should eat. I grew up with six brothers and sisters and we ate whatever and whenever they put food on the table. I was used to eating. Diet? Who diets? Even if there were overweight people in the family, they never dieted. They just never thought they had a weight problem, and they weren't about to starve themselves.

"I didn't change my eating habits until I was in my second year of college, when I went to Italy. I had started with exercise, rhythm and dance, so I was able to eat and eat. I went to Italy with my school in the summer, and the ladies who saw me were amazed at my height and how thin I was, and they admired my tan.

"'How do you stay so beautiful?' they asked. They became very attached to this skinny boy from the United States. 'We are going to feed you, we are going to make you fat.' So they fed me. . . .

"They fed me what I loved best, spaghetti and macaroni and all of the other pastas. I didn't know any better so I thought, I'll just eat it this summer. . . ."

Mel laughs. "Not only did I continue to get taller, but I expanded my shoulders, my legs got some weight on them and I had what I figured were muscles. I said to myself, 'I'm growing!'

"I continued to eat, and I kept growing and growing. Finally, I just couldn't stand it anymore. But I couldn't stop." He goes on to explain how he finally discovered the importance of weight control. "Then, one day, I missed two meals because I was working hard in school just before graduating. I had missed lunch and dinner and I went to bed hungry that night. But in the morning, I jumped on the scale and found that I'd lost five pounds. I finally realized that if I didn't eat, I'd lose weight!

"I started trying to diet and started *thinking* about the things I was eating."

Dancers seem to come by their appreciation of weight control and sensible eating habits through hard experience. Many tell of impossible diets, or uncontrollable eating binges, or guaranteed weight plans that never seem to work.

Merrill Ashley describes her own search for a diet that works. "I have always been bad at dieting. When I heard about a doctor who had helped a friend of mine stop smoking and another to lose weight, I thought it was worth a try.

"It turned out to be a form of acupuncture. I thought what I was going to get were needles that would suppress my appetite so I wouldn't want to eat. What they didn't tell me was that you were required to go on a diet as well. . . ." Merrill grimaces and laughs. "So, I went there and he said, 'Here are the needles and here is a thousand-calorie-a-day diet.' And I thought, Oh, no! No wonder you lose weight, because if I could stick to a thousand-calorie-a-day diet, I would have no trouble losing weight in the first place!

"Well, the needles do make it easier," she explains. "It didn't help the hunger so much, even though he said that every time I felt hungry I should rub them a little bit. But what I found was that when I did eat, I was satisfied much sooner. I felt full after eating, so the needles were helpful—they definitely helped."

It may be that the acupuncture sessions helped Merrill stick to the thousand-calorie-a-day diet, but whether it was because of the needles, or just because Merrill had committed herself to the diet, is difficult to say.

Peter Fonseca talks about other methods that have found favor among dancers at one time or another. "I've tried lots of foods. I've tried to eat sushi, I've tried to eat health foods, I've tried eating an all-natural diet.

"What I've found more than anything else [about people who swear by such diets] is that they will always go to extremes rather than find something that works on a regular basis. They'll go two days without eating a thing and then all of a sudden they just can't stand it anymore, and they break down and pig out. They just blow right up."

The starving and then overindulging syndrome is one that several dancers comment on. Marika Molnar is exasperated by it, and finds that dancers tend to snack when they're on extreme diets. "I'm always seeing them with some little tidbit or cookie or something else. And worse, there is always all that food in the theater. People know we have to be thin, but they are always sending us cookies and cakes. I will never understand it."

As we discussed in Chapters Three and Four, any diet that prevents you from developing natural and healthful eating habits is one that has built-in problems. Too often the tendency is to swing too far the other way in compensating for a restricted diet, whether it's snacking on the sly, or gorging after a fast, or even trying to get back to normal after unusual eating habits.

"One time when I was injured, I didn't gain weight because I went on the Scarsdale diet," says Cynthia Harvey. "It worked . . . it really worked. I followed it to the letter. . . . Boring, though. Any of those diets are too boring for me."

Boring is the right word for it. And on a boring diet, you find that you can't think about anything else but food, which foods you're going to eat next and which foods you've got to deny yourself.

I remember one summer when my daughter figured out that we ate thirty-five watermelons and a hundred pounds of cottage cheese!

Muriel Stuart is much wiser than that. When I said, "It's the style to be thinner today than it used to be," Muriel answered, "Yes, but to anyone who is intelligent, who cares about what style it is today? I mean, if I were to go about doing the things that we're being told to do today, I would lose my mind! Nothing too extreme is good. But unfortunately, that's the trouble with young dancers."

It's true that there is a certain peer pressure in ballet schools and companies that makes young dancers overly conscious of weight and dieting. To be successful dancers, however, they must also learn which foods are vital for health and energy.

"It's so hard to follow a diet," says Jean-Pierre Bonnefous, "that some dancers who do diet simply don't eat for one or two days."

"I think we do too much of the extreme," Patty McBride warns. "If only we could know better. I think this book is as much for dancers as it is for the public!"

Any young dancer who imagines she will get ahead in ballet by extreme dieting or by maintaining an unhealthily low weight, even before reaching the point of the psychological disturbance known as anorexia nervosa, is dangerously naive and disastrously uninformed. A dancer's first goal *must* be to maintain her health and strength, before she worries about trimming pounds or inches.

Most dancers will agree, a well-balanced diet, such as one that follows the menus in the previous chapter, is far more practical than tofu, or watermelon, or padlocks!

Patricia McBride and Conrad Ludlow of NYCB in *Ballet Imperial* by George Balanchine. *(Photo copyright © 1983 by Martha Swope)*

CHAPTER SEVEN
Ballet, the Oldest
Beauty Exercise

Suzanne Farrell is adamant on the subject. "I think everyone should take ballet classes.

"I know that not everyone wants to be a dancer, but if you are interested in staying in good shape, physically and mentally, for a long time, you should just take ballet class as often as you can.

"It's much better than jogging. When you're jogging, your mind is somewhere else, and you're not even relaxed mentally. When you run, you are just using energy and getting more tense and tired.

"But with ballet, it doesn't matter if your execution is awful. The whole idea is that *you* are mentally in control. *You* say, 'All right, leg, développés. All right, now turn.' You are in total control and this is not true of most sports. It gives you a sense of power."

Perhaps it's not surprising that a professional dancer is so high on the benefits of ballet, but when a beautiful ballerina like Suzanne talks about staying in shape, a lot of people will want to listen.

Without a doubt, ballet has one of the oldest pedigrees of all beauty exercises. Its basic structure and many of its positions date back more than two hundred years. Its movements have evolved as forms that enhance the grace and beauty of the dancers. The ballet seen today is the result of centuries of learning how a dancer's body can be made strong and supple while capable of expressing the qualities of lyricism and delicacy.

Suzanne Farrell at age nineteen with George Balanchine, Anthony Blum, and Richard Rapp. *(Photo copyright © 1983 by Martha Swope)*

Ballet classes have one true goal: to produce a beautiful product. It is just about the only controlled exercise in which beauty is the primary goal, and agility and strength are of secondary importance. A dancer will always be working for speed, height or stamina, but her first concern is to look good while doing it. In ballet, form is everything.

Ballet tones up the body. It requires you to stand and move in a particularly balanced way. It benefits your coordination, your posture, your flexibility and your emotional well-being.

As Jacques D'Amboise, a star of the New York City Ballet, of the Broadway stage and of Hollywood, says, "I recommend dance for health. I recommend music and I recommend change, and people should do it now because it is not too late. If they didn't do it when they were young, they are sadly uneducated. They missed out on some facts.

"Yes, I do recommend for everybody the arts, and dancing in particular. The most successful type of technique is ballet, and I recommend ballet."

Needless to say, you don't have to be a professional to attend ballet class, or to take advantage of it. Amateurs have taken ballet classes almost since ballet was first invented. In fact, King Louis XIV was a devoted dancer and was especially fond of ballets in which he could take part.

Since his time, a great many amateur dancers have looked to ballet for developing a more graceful carriage and improved posture or deportment. One thing is certain, you stand up straight when you're in a ballet class. What's more, word is getting around that ballet can also be a dynamic and challenging form of exercise. Without aspiring to a professional dance career, people seeking a beautiful and rewarding form of exercise seem to be turning to ballet classes more than ever before.

This is not to say that ballet is the only kind of recreation that is good for you. But ballet is unique in that it is a structured exercise that emphasizes form and grace. And as if that weren't enough to recommend it, it's all done to a background of beautiful music.

Of her own introduction to ballet training, Madame Danilova tells us about how "in Russia, in every establishment, they would give a Christmas party. So when I was a little girl in school, they gave a performance for Christmas. In every school at that time, we had ballroom dancing, music lessons, choir practice, and so on. For the Christmas performance I was told to be a butterfly and fly around the garden. So, I fly around and everybody said, 'Oh, how graceful! You must be a ballerina!' And this I decided: 'Okay, I be a ballerina. . . .'"

The attractions of a life in ballet appeal to many, although individual dancers value different aspects of it. For example, Mel Tomlinson says, "I chose ballet because it was by far the hardest. The techniques you study are more difficult and demanding and I thought that it would aid me in life as well.

"I was seventeen when I made the decision [to become a dancer], which is really very late in life. As a kid, I had been the jack of all trades—I had no direction in life. I was into drama and in choirs. I was used to performing in front of people and I loved acting, but it was the movement in ballet that was new to me.

"Actually, I came to ballet at nineteen after two years of modern dance. My whole life changed with ballet."

In terms of physical exertion ballet is strenuous and intensive, and can improve cardiovascular fitness, flexibility and coordination. It emphasizes graceful and beautiful movements; it requires good posture; it strengthens leg, back and arm muscles. It's structured so that everyone, from beginners to veterans, will find challenges in mastering its techniques. And, perhaps the most satisfying element of it is dancing to music—a basic human response. Ballet is first and foremost an art form. It is treasured by lovers of beauty around the world.

"I was performing when I was twelve years old," says Jacques

D'Amboise. "It was really great . . . it transformed my life, and I am now involved in attempting to bring the same thing to other children. Children in general, but boys in particular, should be involved with the arts, but what's crucial is that they should not just witness it, but *participate* in it. You don't learn anything without doing it.

"Dance is a very wonderful, immediate art. After all, anybody can do a knee bend. So I have gotten involved in the pleasure of getting children to dance.

"My classes for city policemen came about because of a fluke, but it happened in order to impress and inspire the young people that dancing was a fantastic cultural thing. I wanted them to perform with great ballet stars, with great stars of the theater, of drama, and music, and to have a whole bunch of New York City cops dancing with them was, I thought, a wonderful expression of love and art . . . the idea of presenting the arts and society as all being one and the same. The arts are universal."

Participating in a beautiful art form is certainly not the least of ballet's attractions, especially to nonprofessionals. One amateur who takes ballet class for recreation told me, "Taking the class helps me watch ballet performances from a technical point of view. Not that I had missed the most important parts before, but I have developed a canny sense of what is difficult and what isn't. I also now know what dancers are talking about. . . .

"The music is another big plus. Besides the fact that ballet is so hard to get right, music makes it the only form of exercise that isn't boring."

Edward Villella describes ballet as "a lovely investigation. First, it's an investigation of our physicality, and gives us a sense of our bodies. It gives us two things, really, it gives us an interior sense of our bodies and also gives us an outward sense of our bodies, because that is what dancing is all about: line and form, and the movement of that line and form with relation to time and space.

NYCB's Edward Villella in *Watermill* by Jerome Robbins. *(Photo copyright © 1983 by Martha Swope)*

"So dancing gives you an overall view of the outline of your body while you are looking from the inside out. What separates it from other normal, so-called investigations of physicality is that this is a *total* investigation of the entire body working simultaneously, and yet isolating levels of energy. It's a very, very sophisticated view of the physical, probably more so than almost any other form of physical activity, other than, say, Olympic gymnastics.

"In other words, it's not just an investigation of the performance of three or four or five special feats, it's a total investigation of the body through what I like to refer to as the supportive gesture. For example, if you lift an arm, it's not just your shoulder that's lifting your arm. The dancer thinks about it as the entire body supporting the lifting of that arm.

"Ballet is obviously all based on the turn-out [the essential posture of the ballet dancer: torso erect with the legs, from the hips down, turned outward], because the turn-out is what supports energy.

"You are rotating up and away and out all the time. That gives a kind of column-type support, from the right shoulder all the way down the legs to the right toes, and the same on the left side. But you are using the whole body with that kind of rotating structural support.

"Athletics don't have that kind of investigation," he continues. "If you're a baseball pitcher, for example, the arm that you pitch with, the push-off leg and the landing leg are the extent of your physical investigation. Dancers wouldn't think about just those one or two gestures, but about the movement of the entire body."

"Dancers are athletes of the arts, really," adds Jacques D'Amboise. "Dancers have a discipline of constantly working on themselves, toward achieving a goal. Gymnasts are similar, but they have only a certain length of time in which to perform, and during the time they're at their peak, their bodies are built. They are also very disciplined in terms of exercise.

"The key thing is to believe that the *achievement* of goals is not that important. It's the process of *attempting* to achieve the goals that should be primary.

"The final goal should not be the major concern. After all, we can only control things on a day-to-day basis. I'll give you an example: You plan to dance *Swan Lake* at a Kennedy Center benefit for heads of state on such and such a date. You work all year for that—you talk about it, see everybody, read everything, you practice, you rehearse, you do everything possible. Then the day comes, and there's a strike and the performance is canceled. You never get a chance to do that fantastic *Swan Lake* you were supposed to do on that date. But you've transformed yourself, you're a fantastic Odette, because you've done all the work for it.

"So, I think I would say, enjoy the process of learning to dance. The *process* of our profession, and not its final achievement, is the heart and soul of the dance. Because time and circumstances decide the facts, not you."

"You get form out of ballet," says Suzanne Farrell. "You can develop different areas of your body, because you work over each of these areas.

"A lot of people are not in control of *any* area of their lives. So it's up to you; if you take a ballet class, you can come away feeling good."

When she talks about feeling good, Suzanne is referring not only to the feeling of control over your body, but also to a sense of physical and mental well-being that comes with ballet training. Many dancers, professional as well as amateur, testify to the health-improvement benefits derived from taking class regularly. One nonprofessional exclaims, "It's a great tension reliever, and cheaper than a psychiatrist!"

You go to class, become absorbed in its intricate structure and say, "Oh, no, it's not right! Well, I'm going to make it right!" You find you're never satisfied, and by the end of the class you have exhausted all of your craziness, your neuroses or your nervous intensity. You definitely feel better when you leave your dance class—it's therapeutic, and certainly very far from an office or a counter or a desk.

And the great advantage of ballet is that you don't have to worry about whether you're young or old in order to participate. Dancing can help keep you young through its constant challenge and activity.

"My back is stronger, my knee doesn't hurt me and my ankles are less fragile because my feet are stronger," explains a nonprofessional devotee of ballet classes. "From an orthopedic point of view, I am very much healthier. Conversely, when I don't take class for a couple of weeks, all of the old aches and pains come back. It's really so crucial for my health, I feel I should try to write off the cost on my income tax!"

Marika Molnar agrees. "That's true. Most people rarely complain about anything when they're dancing. It's after they've stopped dancing that they start to feel some aches and pains."

This is not to say that ballet is an either-or proposition, that you must devote the rest of your life to ballet class or you'll start feeling bad the minute you stop. Rather, that you feel good when you're dancing, and an interruption of it makes you more sensitive to the dull aches and pains of inactivity. In some cases ballet training has even been known to prevent or mitigate injury. "Back in California, my teacher had been in a very bad accident," says Cynthia Harvey. "The doctor told her that anyone else would have broken her neck, but her strength as a dancer had prevented such serious injury."

Certainly ballet class is not the cure for all ailments, or a surefire tonic for good health. Ballet training may be too strenuous or stressful for many people. Of course, the stress of certain ballet movements can be great, even for veteran dancers. But then, anything can be harmful or wrong if it's approached in the wrong way. Ballet must be a *supervised* exercise, and it's important to get the right supervision as well. But it is an excellent, satisfying form of exercise and recreation for people who enjoy

Susan Freedman of NYCB in company class at the Kennedy Center in Washington, D.C. *(Photo copyright by Steven Caras)*

movement to music, or for anyone in search of a structured physical activity.

"I am very competitive in my professional life, so ballet class is one area where I don't really have to be competitive," says one nonprofessional student. "The nice thing about starting ballet [later in life] is that there are no fantasies, and that's very relaxing for me. I'm glad, really, that I didn't start until middle age. I started two and a half years ago, when I was thirty-nine. Before that, I'd taken modern dance for a year or so and that was really the first time I'd taken any dance training at all.

"I changed to ballet classes because I wanted better placement [correct posture and positioning] for modern dance, but as I took ballet, it just became more interesting to me. I also realized that it was the healthiest form of dance and exercise for my own body.

"I have a tendency toward weak ankles, and a slipped disc, and I found I had to do some sort of activity that is very controlled. One doesn't have control over oneself in, say, a tennis game. I think the ultimate sport is to be a ballerina!

"Frankly, I just got hooked on ballet. It's such a rigorous form of exercise, and the more classes you take, the more you want to continue taking it—and the better you feel.

"The thing about ballet that's like tennis or running is that no matter where you go, you can do it. You can find a ballet studio anywhere. I experimented once when I was in London for a conference. Although I was only there for three days, I wanted to see what a ballet class there was like. I found a marvelous studio near Covent Garden and was perfectly happy."

My friend concludes, "I like the things that go with ballet. I like being hot, I hate being cold. In wintertime I know that six times a week I can be guaranteed that I'll be really warm for an hour and a half."

Ballet class does have that advantage. It takes place indoors, and because it's a group form of exercise, it's easier to keep your commitment to it. There is a built-in, or institutional, discipline that you can latch onto, whereas an activity like jogging is a solitary one that you may have to force yourself to stay with, day in and day out through heat waves and snowstorms. At least in a ballet class it's warm and dry and friendly.

Almost any dance class will provide the activity and recreation that Rule Three of the Dancers' Diet requires. For many, the unstructured freedom of exercise to music will be enough. To many others, however, ballet's classic tradition is of enormous appeal.

Choosing the right class is essential of course.

How does a non-dancer go about finding a ballet class—one that will bring a beginner along gently yet provide a challenge?

First of all, it must be very carefully supervised, with an experienced instructor who is present at all times. Beginners should never be allowed to attempt positions that are so strenuous that they are painful, and it is up to the instructor to make this very clear to the students.

As Muriel Stuart explains, "Every position we take is fighting nature. That is what makes the beauty of ballet, and that's why it is hideous if it isn't beautifully done. *Never, never, never force!*"

The first lesson of ballet deals with posture, which must always be very straight, with the stomach pulled in, the buttocks tucked under, the shoulders down, and the legs turned out from the hip joints (*never* force your feet into a turned-out position). A ballet dancer works to widen the turn-out of the feet from a 90° angle to one that is virtually 180°. However, beginners, especially adult beginners, must be satisfied with a 90° turn-out and can hurt themselves by attempting to force a wider angle.

Dancers who begin their training as children are often able to develop the 180° turn-out expected of professional dancers. Someone who begins as an adult, however, will only strain or injure his or her leg muscles by attempting to develop such an angle. Even professionals must be careful not to exaggerate the turn-out—at a crazy 195°, the Achilles tendons and knees are going to be dangerously strained.

The warnings about what a beginning dance student should and should not attempt must come from the teacher. No one should enter a ballet class with preconceived notions about what ballerinas do to look like ballerinas. Those ideas about toe shoes, wide-open turn-outs or crazy leg splits should be left with children's books about ballet.

Marika Molnar warns, "A lot of the responsibility falls on the teacher, but also on the dancer in terms of knowing what type of class she's going to and what she expects to get out of a class.

"You have lots of problems stemming from early age if a teacher has let the student wear point shoes too early. I think, for instance, that the School of American Ballet has set a good standard by not allowing children on point until they are at least eleven years of age, or at least before they've had a certain number of years of training. Allowing children to go on point well before the bones are actually formed enough to stand the stress causes a lot of the injuries you see in the sixteen-year-old who went on point at the age of eight."

That warning is critical for any young dance student. An adult beginner probably won't want to consider using toe shoes at all. There is no need for an amateur to try to develop a point technique. All dancing done in a ballet class can be done in soft ballet slippers. Most nonprofessional dancers feel that no one in her right mind would attempt to punish her aching feet by cramming them into toe shoes and then pirouetting on them—no one, that is, but a ballerina.

Marika goes on to describe what she feels is the ideal environment for dance classes. "I feel the environment should be more controlled, even so far as ensuring that everyone has the correct size shoes. If every floor were a perfect floor. If nobody had to dance on a hard floor. If there were no slippery floors. If the music were always played the right way. If all these outside en-

ABT feet in *tendu* at the barre. *(Photo copyright by Steven Caras)*

vironmental things could be under control, then I think that the four to six hours that dancers put in daily would not be so over-powering.

"I personally think that pre-barre exercises should be optional, but everybody who goes into a class should know the few things that need to be done before the class starts. For example, there are some very good exercises for people who are constantly straining their feet. Before even putting on the slippers, they should put their feet on the ground without weight and just warm up the toes through the extension of the tendons all across the top of the foot. Warm up the toes, and then warm up the arches. This probably wouldn't take more than ten minutes for the whole thing.

"And before even putting on your slippers, you should lie down on the floor and warm up the hip joint by doing circular rotations of the hip. This way your body is getting a little warm and more receptive to going through the nice, slow barre movements. It should begin slowly with an *andante* tempo and then become gradually faster, until you leave the barre and do all the center work without it. It should all be done the same way, starting slowly and then progressing to faster things.

"After it's all said and done, then you work up to actually moving across the floor and dancing. That, I think, is the proper progression for a class. Then every part of your body has had a chance to go through a progression of movement, having first been properly warmed up."

If you do decide that ballet class is what you would like to take advantage of in making your own life more active, keep in mind the following advice:

- Before signing up for an expensive course of classes, before going out and buying designer warm-up clothes, speak to the ballet studios in your area about what is offered to an adult beginner. Make sure that the schedule of classes is one that is convenient, that instructor supervision is an important part of the class and that the facilities are really proper for the training given.

· Start out with a simple leotard, tights, and a pair of dance slippers. In cold or clammy weather, you may want to consider leg warmers, which help prevent strains and cramps. Be comfortable in your clothes, and don't worry so much about appearance. Find a way to keep your hair back and out of your face.

· *Never overdo.* Don't push your body when it's telling you that it hurts, and don't expect to accomplish dazzling feats of flexibility and strength without a slow, cautious development of your physical abilities. Remember that ballet class is supposed to be recreation and that there is no need to compete with anyone except yourself. One of the great advantages of ballet training is that you can develop your own abilities at the pace most suitable for you. Forcing things, whether it's turn-out or extension, can only result in pain and injury.

· Finally, enjoy it! Dancing is one of life's most enjoyable experiences, and ballet is one of its most beautiful.

CHAPTER EIGHT
Dancers' Serious Exercise

Many professional dancers supplement traditional ballet classes with various exercise programs designed to work specific muscles and muscle groups in controlled, scientific ways, in order to increase strength and flexibility.

Whether you are a dancer, or an athlete, or simply interested in keeping your body fit, there are several important things to keep in mind when you decide to undertake a serious conditioning program of this kind.

The first question to ask is: What do you really want to get out of conditioning exercises? For the dancer, it's important to pursue exercises that not only enhance technique and ability, but maintain the dancer's line. A dancer's conditioning course must also utilize the muscles that are neglected through ballet training, while making sure that muscles vital to ballet technique are not strained or stressed.

As therapist of the New York City Ballet, Marika Molnar brings an invaluable insight into dancers' conditioning, both in the ballet class and in the training studio. "Exercises should utilize muscle groups that aren't really used that much during the dancer's everyday activity," she explains.

"I feel strongly that if these muscles are also active, the dancer will not then develop an overuse syndrome, which happens because dancers are constantly in a turned-out position, whether they're in class or rehearsal or even walking on the street (a lot

NYCB's Peter Martins, who confesses to eating junk food—
occasionally. (Photo copyright © 1983 by Martha Swope)

of dancers walk with their feet turned out, which is a very bad habit).

"The dancer should take the time during the day when she is not dancing to use muscles the way muscles are meant to be used—all over the body, the head joints, knee joints, ankle joints. There should be a time of day when dancers are not constantly stretching the same group of muscles over and over again. There are certain groups of exercises that are vital to get other muscles into action and not let them take a secondary position. It can also make the body aware that it has these other muscles as well and can call upon them when needed to take a little stress off the overused muscles."

Marika goes on to discuss one of the most crucial, yet probably most misunderstood, adjuncts to exercise. "People don't really know how to stretch. Every time I go to the park actually, I see the 'bouncers.' Almost everyone does it unfortunately. You know, people attempt to stretch before exercising, the way they see others do it, not necessarily finding out how it's properly done.

"So you see the joggers running around the park, the roller skaters, the tennis players, even professional athletes will run out, stick out their rear ends and bounce forward a few times. Millions of people watch these athletes on television, thinking that because they're professionals they must know how to stretch. You know, people think that is the way to start exercising. They just don't bother to find out what the proper way is.

"Stretching the muscles," she continues, "is something that's essential. It's important, not just for dancers, but for anybody who spends a lot of time and energy in any physical activity, to stretch before and after exercising. The best time to stretch, the most effective and beneficial time to reduce muscle soreness and to increase the length of the muscle, is after you are really warmed up.

"For example, I make the case that if anybody and everybody took five to ten minutes to stretch the sides of their bodies and their calves *after* class, the people who have problems with calves and Achilles tendons particularly would save themselves so much trouble. I've seen it happen so often: They 'solve' all their problems by taking three minutes during a rehearsal or after a performance or standing around bored by doing an Achilles-tendon stretch.

"It would save them so much trouble for the future and it immediately saves them for the next day. Instead of being sore, they feel fine and have no problems, because the stretching helps get rid of the built-up waste products that accumulate when you overuse the muscle. With sports medicine now becoming such a big thing, this is now being taught to physical educators and doctors."

According to Marika, many ballet-related injuries or simple aches and pains may be avoided by proper stretching techniques. Even muscle spasms or cramps are related to muscles that are inadequately conditioned before and after activity. "The best thing to do for a sudden spasm or cramping is to stretch out that muscle immediately. If you're performing, unfortunately, you can't do that. But if, for example, you have a cramp in the calf muscle, sit down as soon as possible and half pull and half stretch it. Stretch your foot up toward you, flex your foot for a minute or two, and that will almost immediately relieve the tension. Many people will do this unconsciously. Say you're sitting down, off your feet for a moment, and are doing some pointing and flexing. All of a sudden you get a cramp in the bottom of the foot. Most people will stand up and walk around and that will get rid of it. What you're doing basically is stretching out the sole of the foot, all the little muscles that are in your foot are being stretched. The same thing goes for any place on your body where you feel a cramp coming on. Ice can also help that kind of cramp because it slightly anesthetizes the area."

Marika goes on to explain and demonstrate the rules for proper stretching. A common misconception is that bouncing while reaching or extending will stretch the muscles adequately.

Lauren Hauser of NYCB stretching in arabesque at the barre. (*Photo copyright by Steven Caras*)

Not so, says Marika. "Stretching should be done *statically*, which means that you find and isolate the muscle group that you want to stretch. For example, when you stretch the hamstring area and you feel a little soreness in the back of your legs, which is where the hamstrings are located, you must get to that point and not any farther. You stay at that point for a minimum of thirty seconds so that the muscle and tendon and all the sensor organs (which allow you to tone the muscles and tendons) adapt to the new rank. And then the muscle can be relaxed and stretched forward.

"But if you constantly bounce up and down, the muscle and/or tendon doesn't get a chance to adapt and is, in reality, constantly being shortened. That is called the stretch reflex—it is really doing the opposite of what you want.

"Another mistake people make," Marika continues, "is to believe that you have to have severe pain in order to be really stretching, but that's not the case. You should just feel the muscle being stretched a little, and then stop. Don't go to the point where your back is killing you and you feel that any minute the tendon is going to pop off the bone. That's *not* going to help you."

Keeping these admonitions in mind, anyone who makes the decision to pursue a course of serious exercise should do the research necessary to select a program that will provide the proper results. While dancers require programs that will offset ballet-related problems and, at the same time, enhance strength and flexibility, others who are not professional dancers may seek programs that can relieve tension, or develop special muscle groups or trim physical proportions.

Serious exercise programs or therapeutic programs must, above all, be *supervised* activities. This does not just mean that an attendant shows you the facilities or demonstrates the apparatus, but that a qualified assistant works with you to set goals and develop programs that address those goals and to monitor your activities and your progress.

Nautilus, one of the most popular of the serious exercise pro-grams, features resistance machines operated by cam action, a system of weights and springs, that is used to strengthen specific areas of the body in a controlled, systematic way. While supervi-sion is required with the Nautilus method, the attendant or su-pervisor does not interact with the subject during the actual exercise. Similar methods can be found in gymnasiums, health clubs, spas, Y's and body-building establishments.

Dancers are constantly investigating alternative means of en-hancing their performances, and successful methods quickly become popular in ballet circles through word-of-mouth recom-mendations. One program that seems ideally suited to many dancers' needs, and is extremely popular with professional and nonprofessional dancers alike, is known as the Pilates Method. Pilates, in comparison with the Nautilus method, employs a pas-sive apparatus where the positioning of the user is all-important. In this case, it is the supervisor who determines the positioning, the exercise and the resistance, if any, and who will ultimately determine the degree of the user's success with Pilates. Because this form of exercise can't be practiced independently, there is an added safety factor.

In pursuing this subject, I spoke with Mary Kasakove, a part-ner of the Anderson-Kasakove Studio, Inc., located a few blocks from Lincoln Center in New York City. Anderson-Kasakove of-fers personalized exercise programs based on the Pilates Method, and is so popular with New York dancers that Mary likes to joke that she could start her own ballet company, and have more stars in it than any other.

"Pilates is a method of exercise invented by Joseph Pilates about fifty years ago," explains Mary. "He invented specific ex-ercises with equipment to go with them. His belief was that it was healthy for people to work against resistance. He felt that it activated muscles very efficiently and helped people get a good feel of those muscles.

"There are some muscles that are hard to work on, even when

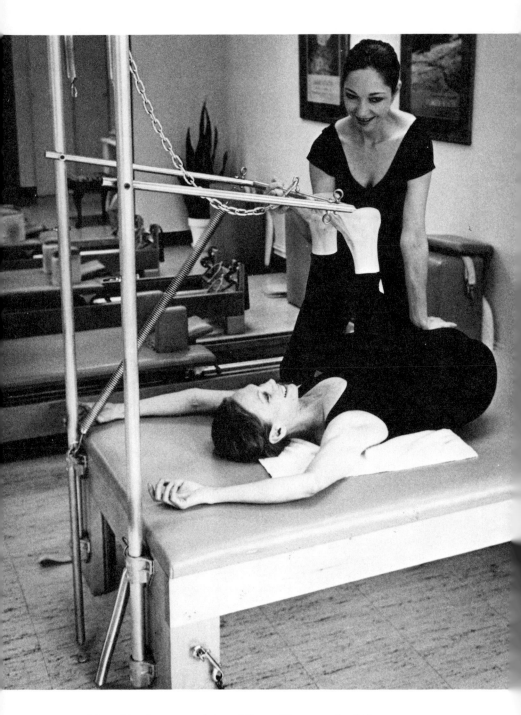

Mary Kasakove coaching Allegra Kent on the Pilates apparatus. Shown here is the lowest part of "The Tower," which stretches the hamstrings. (*Photo copyright © 1983 by James J. Camner*)

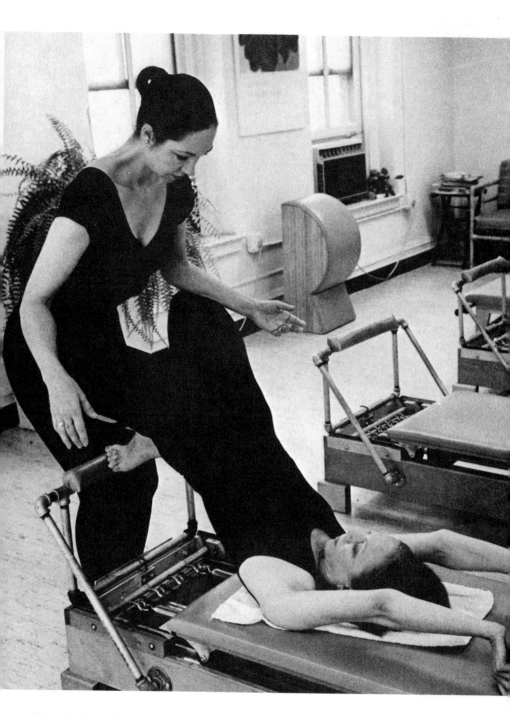

Mary helps Allegra with "The Semicircles." (*Photo copyright © 1983 by James J. Camner*)

you are working them correctly. You just don't feel them: the inner thighs, the back of the thighs, the back of your arms. So the resistance type of exercises on this equipment," she says, pointing to the various pieces of equipment in the studio, "make it very easy to isolate the different muscle groups. And most of the exercises are done lying down, so they are safe. The back is supported and the neck is supported, and you can concentrate on the area you want to work on.

"Another advantage," Mary continues, "is that the apparatus can be adjusted to just the level of challenge your body can take. You can work very methodically, which is very useful for dancers because in class you compete and keep up with the music, you watch the girl ahead of you and try to match her or be better. With these exercises, you can come back to a more natural form of movement and fill in the gaps that dancing leaves. You also strengthen your strengths."

The Pilates Method helps to compensate for the "overuse syndrome" that Marika Molnar mentioned earlier. Explaining that a dancer can't rely on the strong muscle groups developed in ballet when working out on the Pilates apparatus, Mary notes that "with this type of exercise, you are placed in the right position and monitored. If the right muscles aren't being used, you can't move. You can't compensate with momentum or with speed or with other parts of the body."

She also emphasizes the importance of careful supervision when using the equipment. "There is always a potential for someone to do something she shouldn't. We try to stay close to people and schedule our sessions so that our clients get individual attention. This is an advantage for the top-notch dancers especially. That's because when they reach a certain level in an advanced ballet class, they find they are placed in the front of the room like a showpiece and may not necessarily be corrected as they would like to be.

"I would definitely recommend these exercises for beginners as well. We have people of all levels, all ages from eleven to over

Here Mary coaches Allegra in a stretch that increases back
flexibility. *(Photo copyright © 1983 by James J. Camner)*

sixty-five, dancers and non-dancers, physical and nonphysical people. I think Pilates is ideal for anyone who has never exercised, and can help someone like that get a feel for the body. Even if they don't stay with it, you have given them a background—they know they have a body to work with."

Nevertheless, Mary warns that the Pilates Method is not a substitute for physical therapy. "I would like to think of it as a kind of intermediate step, between the doctor and therapist and the dancer's everyday activity. When someone comes to us with an injury to work on, we generally call the doctor to get permission to work with the client, and to find out what we should and shouldn't do.

"We get a lot of joggers and a lot of tennis players besides dancers," she says. "We even get some movie stars. You might find it surprising, but because of our proximity to Lincoln Center, we get musicians who come in with neck and shoulder problems from sawing away at a cello or waving a baton. It's all the same, really.

"We're different from other equipment-type programs that also work with the resistance principle. Because Pilates is so adaptable, you can work out something for everybody. I think that it's a much more adaptable, interesting and human method."

Jacques D'Amboise is one of the Pilates program's most vocal proponents. "I very much believe in Pilates," he says. "I believe it's wonderful—just the best form of exercise in the entire world. Nothing is better."

Peter Fonseca says, "It's really preventive medicine for injuries and things like that. They [the Pilates supervisors] are very good at picking out a weakness that you might not otherwise be aware of. The attendants see you on the machines and can say right away, 'Your left ankle is weak,' or 'Strengthen the whole leg so that you don't strain it.'"

At sixteen, Dierdre Carberry is a devotee of the program. "I go once a week," she confides. "It keeps your body even and straight."

"It was a total toning of the body," says Edward Villella in describing how Pilates helped him come back from an injury. "What was important to me was just to keep the circulation going when I had to wait to come back to dance."

However, the Pilates Method is not necessarily beneficial for everyone. Merrill Ashley found that the program did not provide the results she was looking for. "Places would hurt that never hurt any other time. I also just got bored with it." And, as one nonprofessional warns, "It is very serious exercise. If you're not prepared for it, it can floor you."

Of course, no one program is ideal for everyone. It is important to find one that provides you with the elements you, as an individual, need to acquire strength or to condition yourself or to recover from an injury. Pilates is a useful alternative because its apparatus is flexible enough to adapt to individual strengths and weaknesses as required.

Perhaps the major drawback to the Pilates Method for the general public is that it is currently available in only a few cities. Because it is such a highly supervised program, attendants must be fully trained in the principles behind the Pilates Method and are consequently in great demand. "Any time you use equipment there is a potential for harm as well as good," explains Mary Kasakove. "You have to be watched carefully. If someone came to me now and said, 'I want to open up my own studio. Will you train me?', I would say, 'It will take three years at least.'"

The Pilates Method is one good example of a serious exercise program with an individually adaptable form of training. While it is in no way a sport or a recreation, it is an efficient way to obtain specific physical results.

A Pilates or Nautilus method may also be attractive to a nonprofessional in helping him or her to pursue an informal sport like jogging or tennis without stress or injury. If you tend to throw yourself into an activity without taking the precautions necessary to avoid problems, a structured and supervised program may be the answer for you.

Before you undertake a serious exercise program, however, the following recommendations are worth considering:

- Try to analyze exactly what it is you are looking for in a serious program. Is it an overall improvement in strength or flexibility? Or are you addressing specific physical weaknesses or problems?

- Carefully research which programs are available to you, and include in that research discussions with the directors or the attendants about your specific, individual goals. Don't let someone else sell you a program that you don't really need.

- Be serious and committed to the program you select. Allow it enough time to work, and make sure you are giving it your full cooperation.

- Rely on and make use of the person supervising your activities. Make sure you are getting a program specifically tailored to your needs. Reevaluate your progress frequently.

CHAPTER NINE
Fun and Games

If you'll remember, in Chapter Four, the third important rule of the Dancers' Diet is to make exercise and physical activity an important part of your diet.

We've talked about the ways dancers are active: up to six, and sometimes even more, hours every day in class, rehearsal and performance, as well as additional exercise programs. Some dancers look for the serious supervision of the Pilates Method, while others try to spend some time in a swimming pool every day. Dancers try to avoid the sports that place greater risk of injury on certain areas of their bodies, but they are frequently active and avid sports enthusiasts.

In order for you to take advantage of the Dancers' Diet, you must make your life more active. Whether you sign up for ballet classes or make an appointment at your local health spa, or whether you just step out the front door to take a long, brisk walk, exercise and physical activity must be a part of your plans.

To help you select a form of exercise that you will find useful and enjoyable, this chapter will talk about different, less structured, activities you may also consider as ways to improve your activity level gradually yet significantly.

Swimming

"We came from the sea and you realize it the minute you get back in the water," says Jacques D'Amboise. "Swimming is my

165 ·

Allegra Kent synthesizing her two favorite kinds of exercise. *(Photo copyright by Hank O'Neal)*

favorite recreation. If I could have what I wanted, it would be an enormous swimming pool right next to my bed, and I would roll right out of bed in the morning and swim!"

Swimming is an excellent form of exercise because it avoids the danger of serious strain or injury to certain muscles. It's also useful for dancers because it improves upper-body strength and increases stamina while it relieves all pressure on overused muscles in the feet, calves and back. (For those reasons, it is also one of the best exercises for pregnant women.)

Cynthia Harvey also recommends it. "I go swimming whenever I can," she says. "I'm a regular California girl."

Most dancers agree that swimming is an activity that complements ballet training beautifully. It is perhaps the most popular alternate form of exercise among them. It is also an activity that non-dancers can enjoy fully without requiring a tremendous investment of money, time or energy.

Floor Exercises

Floor exercises are those that are done more or less in a stationary position. They can include simple stretches, like knee bends or leg kicks, repeated a few or several times, or they can involve a variety of basic or complicated accessories, like a jump rope or a set of weights. They can be done anywhere and anytime, alone or in a group, by people of all ages. You can do floor exercises by yourself in your own home or you can join a class.

The Pilates Method described in Chapter Eight is a form of floor exercise, elevated to a complex, scientific level. But floor exercises need only be as complicated or as simple as you require.

"Jumping rope is becoming a big thing at ABT," reports Cynthia Harvey. "The boys are jumping rope. Natasha [Makarova] swears by it. Since stamina is my biggest worry, I think it's great. After all, when you're injured or on vacation the first thing you

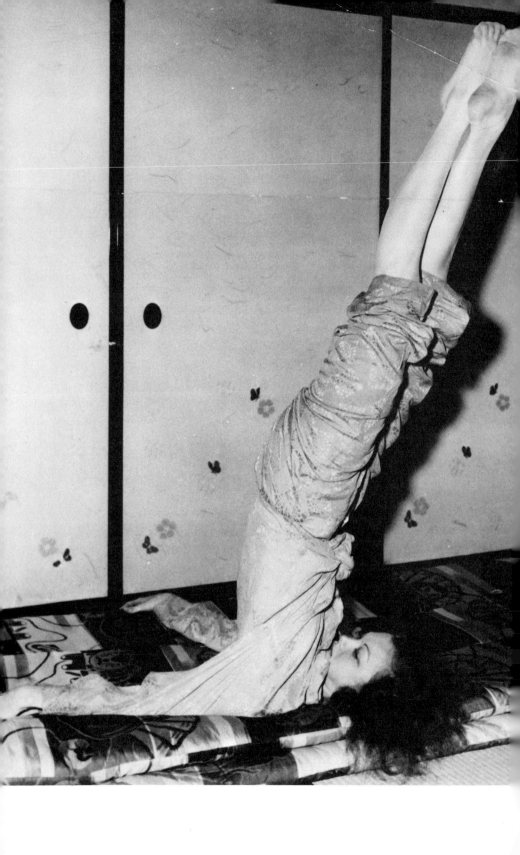

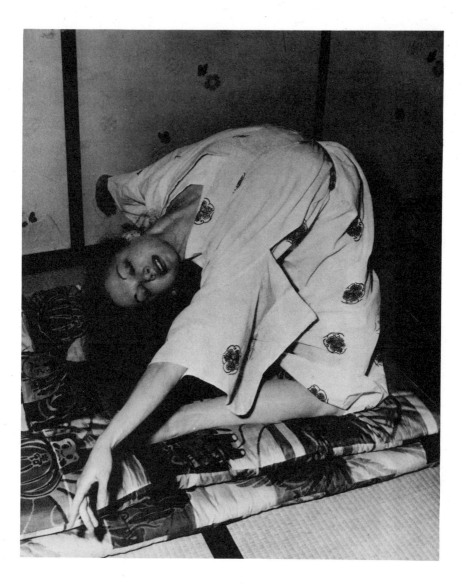

Allegra Kent doing floor exercises in Japan, wearing her pa's pajamas.

notice is that your jump and stamina disappear. Actually, though, it's only with consecutive performances that I find I get back into the best shape."

Marianna Tcherkassky, a principal dancer with American Ballet Theatre, likes to do sit-ups. Peter Fonseca finds that he needs push-ups to improve his upper-body strength. Toni Bentley maintains, "The first thing I do when I get out of bed is a few exercises on the floor just to feel that I'm alive. Every day I do sit-ups until I'm awake."

Muriel Stuart, at the age of eighty, also finds it necessary to go through a series of floor exercises. "I never get out of bed without doing leg exercises twelve times," she says. Merrill Ashley reveals that she prefers exercising with a mat, and likes doing it with a group.

Of course, gymnastics has the ultimate floor exercises. Gymnastics involves a rigorous, strenuous exercise and is great for the figure. Gymnasts, however, also take ballet. . . .

Bicycling

"The bike is good," recommends Isabel Brown. "It's good for your heart. Bike riding is easy and, if you have a stationary bike at home, you can even just watch TV while you're doing it."

A bike is a great piece of exercise equipment, as well as a convenient vehicle of transportation. City biking may be hazardous at times, but it is also one of the only ways to get through a traffic jam. And bike paths are common in many areas of the country.

Bicycling can be a way to get to and from work or school, or it can be a method of touring, biking many miles alone or in a group, or it can be done in a gym, or even without leaving your own living room.

Many people recommend biking for cardiovascular health. In that respect it is superior to jogging, for instance, because it increases the heart rate comparably but does not place the same strain on the feet and legs.

Marika Molnar suggests that people bike at least a half-hour every day. Inside or outdoors, biking steadily for a half-hour or more is an excellent form of exercise for young and old alike.

Walking

Here is one exercise that just about everyone can and should take up. Walking for exercise and recreation is a great way to keep active, stay young and look fit.

Needless to say, walking is available everywhere all the time, and requires no greater investment than half an hour of your time every day. It can be as strenuous as you like, or you can limit your exertion to a gentle stroll, which is why it is a recommended exercise for recovering cardiac patients.

To make walking a rigorous, challenging exercise, however, you must walk briskly for an extended period so that your lungs and your heart are forced to work harder.

To compare calorie-burning properties of various activities, the following figures are helpful:

> Walking 1 ¼ miles in ½ hour—burns approx. 105 calories
> Biking 2 ¾ miles in ½ hour —burns approx. 105 calories
> Walking 2 miles in ½ hour —burns approx. 150 calories
> Biking 6 ½ miles in ½ hour —burns approx. 330 calories
> Running 5 miles in ½ hour —burns approx. 450 calories

The main advantage of walking is that you can do it without even thinking about it: up and down stairs, on errands, after dinner, during your lunch hour. Making a *conscious* effort to do more walking in fact is a very effective way to make your life more active without compelling yourself to take up strenuous exercise.

Walking also is one of the only exercises that doesn't require mastering a skill, and it's almost impossible to injure yourself by walking, unless too-tight shoes give you a blister.

Muriel Stuart maintains that walking has kept her young, and Isabel Brown says, "Walking is essential because it uses your whole body. You're breathing while you walk, your legs are going and your arms and torso move. Fast walking is very good for you."

Ballerinas can often be spotted by their characteristic walk. Training from the start to develop the ideal turn-out, ballerinas find that unless they're careful they will unconsciously turn out their hips, knees and feet even while walking down the street. While their posture is always enviable, dancers should attempt to fight the tendency to turn out, which can be quite harmful to hip and knee joints, except in class or onstage.

Running

Running and jogging are such popular sports that you may have wondered why running is not higher up on the list of dancers' recommended exercises. Most dancers agree, however, that long-distance running and jogging are not kind to dancers.

The pounding of feet on pavement or turf places too great a stress on muscles, bones and tendons of legs and feet. Running may be excellent for toning up the bodies of non-dancers, but shin splints and runners' knees are still common complaints among people who don't put nearly as much daily strain on their legs and feet as dancers are already doing.

Some dancers, Suzanne Farrell among them, object to running because it is an activity that does not place much emphasis

Suzanne Farrell and Jorge Donn in *Nijinsky*. (*Photo copyright by W. Reilly*)

on form or grace. "At least you get some form out of ballet. You can develop different areas because you work every area of your body. When you jog, you're just pumping."

Cynthia Harvey is another dancer who is wary of running. "I don't think it's a good idea. Mainly because it batters the bottoms of your feet. I used to be on the track team in school, but my hamstrings were always sore. Maybe if you had something like space boots . . ."

Jacques D'Amboise is one dancer who jogs regularly, but he is in the minority in this case. Basically, dancers value their calves and feet too highly to attempt to become long-distance runners.

Nevertheless, running is an excellent sport for cardiovascular fitness. It also has the advantage of being available everywhere to just about everybody. While an investment in a good pair of shoes is essential for jogging, it can be taken up with just a sweat shirt and a pair of shorts. It is wrong, however, to think that running can't hurt you: Before starting in, you ought to get the advice of a doctor and learn about how to stretch before running, how to pace yourself and how to know when to stop.

Other Forms of Exercise

"Dancers have to be very careful because we are like an instrument," warns Fernando Bujones. "If you bang a piano too much, you're bound to untune it. If you use your body in other kinds of activities, you may work different muscles or stretch different ligaments. Horseback riding is a perfect example. If you go horseback riding a great deal, there is no way you can go back to ballet and expect to keep the whole thing properly turned out. Weight lifting is all right, a little bit of it, but once again, if you overdo it you're going to end up with muscles that shouldn't be there." Fernando walks, swims or plays tennis for relaxation.

"I had a friend who was in an aerobic dance class at a health club," says Heather Watts when asked what she would recommend as exercise for non-dancers, "and she was doing it for three hours. She said it was like exercising, but that she could wander in and out of the class. She was able to do it and get very limber and strong—she was able to dance through the routines. I liked the fact that people could kind of come in and out of class without difficulty."

There are any number of sports and activities that can offer you a chance to become more active: square dancing, racquetball, volleyball, ice and roller skating, skiing, handball, basketball, hiking, mountain climbing, etc., etc., etc.

Every dieter knows that there are exercise programs for anybody, to be found in books, on television, on video tapes or at the local Y. If you need the motivation of a commitment, don't hesitate to sign up for a group exercise program. However, don't feel you can't participate just as well in the privacy of your own home. The key here is not to let your motivation slip away, but to continue to pursue an exercise program as your way to staying slim and fit.

There is at least one activity that can provide you with just the right combination of factors to make it a part of your life. The important part is that you make it *regular*, a once-a-day habit. The benefits of such a commitment can't be overemphasized.

Some Exercise Programs

Beginner level: choose one

1. Walk everywhere, but take at least a fifteen-minute walk every day.

2. Bicycle, walk fast or swim hard for fifteen minutes, three times a week.

3. Take a one-hour exercise or aerobic dance class once a week.

Intermediate level: choose one

1. Walk half an hour every day.

2. Bicycle, walk fast or swim hard for thirty minutes, at least three times a week.

3. Take a one-hour exercise or aerobic dance class twice a week.

4. Take a ballet class at least once a week.

Advanced level: choose one

1. Walk half an hour every day, in addition to activities #2, #3 and #4 of the intermediate level.

2. Bicycle, walk fast or swim hard for forty-five minutes to an hour, four or more times a week.

3. Have one hour of exercise, aerobic dance or ballet class at least three times a week.

4. Add one session of a serious exercise, such as the Pilates Method, to the activities of the Intermediate level.

Professional level: choose one

1. Engage in an hour of strenuous activity at least five times a week.

2. Add three or more sessions of serious exercise to activities #1, #2 and #3 of the Advanced level.

These four levels of activity should serve as a guide to you as you set about increasing the amount of exercise you get.

For most people starting at the Beginner level, just to work up to the Intermediate level is a sufficient goal. Combined with the Dancers' Diet, both the Beginner and Intermediate levels will be helpful in toning you up as you begin to lose a significant amount of weight.

If you are not currently an active person, start by selecting any one of the three activities listed under the Beginner level. Continue with it, *faithfully*, until it no longer taxes you, either physically or mentally. It may then be time to move up to the Intermediate level. If that level proves too strenuous at first, modify it slightly until it causes you exertion without discomfort.

In this way, you can move up the activity levels at a pace that is just right for you. By all means, feel free to substitute an activity that you enjoy more for the activities listed in these levels.

Remember that you should aim to make these activity levels a part of your life, for the rest of your life. Don't let yourself think they can be maintained for the duration of a diet and then dropped, and still expect to lead a healthy and slender existence. A crucial part of any maintenance diet plan is an elevated level of physical activity.

Provided that your goals are reasonable, that you are careful, that you use common sense and that you make your increased activity a commitment, any one of the four levels will make you feel 100 percent better both physically and mentally.

Needless to say, increasing your level of physical activity also increases your chances for injury. Even dancers, despite their superior conditioning, often suffer pain and injury through carelessness, overwork or just bad luck.

Using common sense is the single most effective way to prevent injury, minor or serious. For heaven's sake, don't bike or jog on a busy street or highway at night; make certain your shoes fit properly, that equipment is in good shape and that facilities are adequate; never push yourself when you feel pain; don't swim where there is no lifeguard; don't attempt feats that are beyond your capabilities; and so on and so on.

Furthermore, it is always a good idea to try to stretch out your muscles before exercising, as Marika Molnar recommends in Chapter Eight. Don't just bounce up and down on your heels for a minute or two—warm yourself up and then stretch slowly, gently and methodically for several minutes. Marika also urges you to stretch *after* your activity, because that's when your muscles are warm and flexible. But never, never stretch until it hurts—just until your muscles are lengthened and relaxed.

Slight soreness is, of course, inevitable when you begin to work muscles that have been inactive, or when you work to strengthen active muscles further. When dancers hurt, they often like to pamper themselves with massage. "I adore being massaged," says Suzanne Farrell. "I love to have my back rubbed, especially my neck to relieve the tension." Baryshnikov swears by massage and indulges in it frequently, and his fellow American Ballet Theatre dancer Cynthia Harvey agrees. "I need to have a massage at least once a week, especially when I'm dancing *Swan Lake* or *Don Q.*"

Suzanne Farrell's other remedies for muscle soreness include cold packs, and wearing heels instead of flats, (which give better support to the calf muscles).

My own recipe for aching muscles is to make giant ice cubes in yogurt cups or plastic storage containers and rub them on my calves. On summer nights, when my calves are especially tired, this ice treatment really helps as I stand over the sink with a wash cloth or glove, rubbing in the ice for four minutes or so.

Marika Molnar also recommends the use of ice packs for tired dancers. "I use a lot of different types of icing techniques. But whatever part of the body I put ice on, I never put it on for more than twenty minutes, because the effect you want will be achieved within twenty minutes. After about half an hour, you start to get a reverse effect, because the superficial blood vessels start to dilate, and the deeper ones start to constrict.

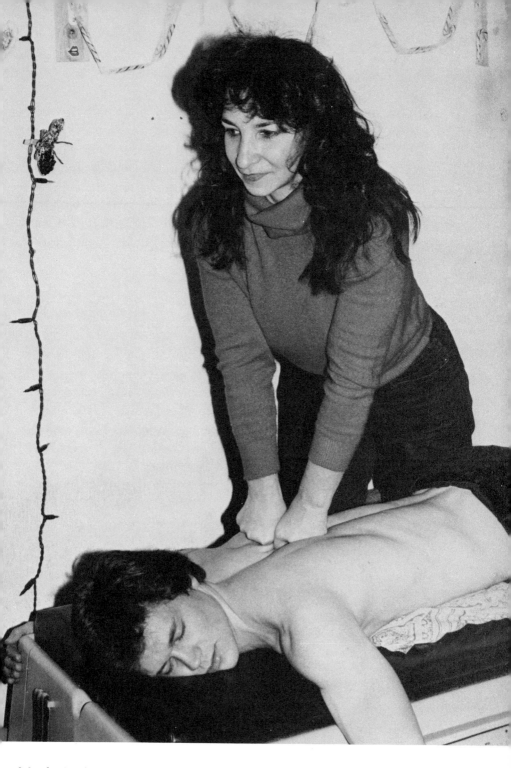

Marika Molnar, physical therapist for NYCB, giving a massage to Joseph Duell. *(Photo copyright by Steven Caras)*

"Ice massages don't need to be done for that length of time, of course. In the case of shin splints in the lower leg, one of the best ways to help prevent it, and also to help treat and rehabilitate it, is to take some ice and rub it up and down your shin until you feel numb. In a way, you are both massaging the area and also anesthetizing it. You go through stages in icing where it starts off feeling cold, then it goes to a burning sensation and an aching sensation, and then numbness. That's where you want to stop icing—when it becomes numb."

So You're Ready to Start

You've made up your mind to start on an exercise program? Good, because that is the most important thing dancers can recommend to the general public. By making your selection from the activity levels of the exercise programs here, and by sticking to it, you can get all the benefits that the dancers have promised.

Here are some points to remember:

- Walk, walk and keep walking.

- Try to make your exercise program a habit, so that you're not constantly having to motivate yourself to get out there and do something.

- Be patient. If you're not used to so much activity you can't become a super-athlete overnight.

- If you are a dancer, you'll want to stick to the activities that Cynthia Harvey calls "pro-dance" exercises, such as swimming, walking, Pilates, etc.

- Before undertaking any strenuous activity, take the

time to warm up and limber up. Use Marika Molnar's stretching techniques (Chapter Eight).

· If you're going to take advantage of an exercise facility, such as a health club or a Nautilus studio, research it before you invest in it. Make certain it offers trained attendants, up-to-date and well-maintained equipment and conditioning apparatus.

· Finally, make the commitment to stick with your increased activity for good—that's the way it will do you the most good!

CHAPTER TEN
A Healthy Outlook

"What is this book about, Allegra?" asks Mikhail Barysh-nikov.

"It's about how dancers stay healthy."

"But I am not healthy . . . I am not built to stay healthy."

"Well, I know you smoke."

"Yes, I smoke, I drink, I don't keep any diet. . . ."

"You're the exception then. You're lucky you don't have to diet. How much do you smoke?"

"I don't smoke in the morning. I start smoking sometimes after twelve, sometimes I have my first cigarette after five o'clock. I haven't had any yet today. Sometimes I smoke half a pack in the evening."

"It depends then?"

"Yes, and sometimes I drink beer and vodka and scotch."

"Okay, but what do you like to eat?"

"I like pasta. I don't like junk food much. I don't care for hamburgers and breads at all. I don't like heavy sauces. I like French food, you know, nouvelle cuisine."

"Do you like to cook?"

"No . . . I like nice food, but it takes a lot of time."

"I know you have no time. What are your favorite foods?"

"Chinese . . . Chinese, and Japanese sashimi and sushi. I like that very much—all fish and Japanese vegetables. I like raw steak . . . good wine . . ."

"How do you react to stress?"

Mikhail Baryshnikov, director of ABT, in *Configurations*. (*Photo copyright © 1983 by Martha Swope*)

"Sometimes I get crazy and sometimes nervous, and I'm scaring people all day, and I get embarrassed. That's my behavior, you know, but I say that I'm sorry . . . sometimes."

"I'd go out of my head . . ."

"No, I'm pretty cool . . . I have to be, or otherwise I would be dead."

"How do you unwind after a performance?"

"I love beer, immediately . . . a couple of beers immediately are just fine, just what I like."

"Do you do any exercises other than ballet?"

"No, not during the week. But during the weekends, when I'm not taking class, I just do some stretching and bending and push-ups and whatever."

"What else do you do?" I asked him.

"I do everything wrong that you are supposed to do."

"Ah, but you're exceptional . . ."

Misha thinks he isn't healthy. That is, he thinks he doesn't follow healthy habits. And yet he is the director of American Ballet Theatre, one of the most important ballet companies in the world, while maintaining a full schedule as a premier dancer. Actually, except for the fact that he smokes, Misha's habits are typical of a dancer, and he is as fit and healthy as anyone else in his company.

Why is it that dancers seem to be healthier than the general public?

They are, for the most part, careful about their health because it directly affects their careers. Most credit their health to their active lives, and nearly every dancer reports that an interruption in a ballet career, for injury or vacation, results in a lessening of that healthy feeling.

There are two famous cases in which people suffering from poor health were advised to take up ballet. As a child in Russia, André Eglevsky, the great premier dancer of the thirties and forties, studied ballet because of his poor health. The famous

American ballerina Nana Gollner studied ballet to regain her strength after suffering from infantile paralysis. Ballet training cannot cure disease but it is a successful way to regain fitness.

"I feel healthy because I am a dancer," explains Fernando Bujones. "I always try to be very careful about my health, though. Because my constitution has always been a very thin one, I have to be careful that I don't overburden it. I have to be very careful that I don't overuse my body and become exhausted, because then I can very easily catch a cold or begin to lose weight."

How to Cope with Stress

A ballet career generates lots of stress: the continual pressure to excel, to compete and to surpass. Stress can be a very destructive force, unfortunately, if it leads to depression, but it can also be a spur to motivation.

Paradoxically, in this line of work, the best way to handle stress is to become *more* involved in working and dancing. I was once told that the best way to cure depression is to keep moving.

Baryshnikov says he tries to stay cool when he finds his work stressful, but other dancers find they need to work, harder if necessary, to overcome the drawbacks of stress.

One nonprofessional describes it very accurately: "This particular form of exercise, dance, is so strenuous that it is the only physical thing that really calms me down. I don't think I could have managed difficult times in my job in the first few years if I hadn't been taking class as often as I was. It has made me a lot more stable and a lot stronger, more able to take the kind of pressure that the job puts on me. In fact, even if I didn't care about what it does for my body physically, I would still continue dancing for stress control.

Fernando Bujones with his wife, Marcia. *(Photo copyright © 1983 by James J. Camner)*

"The whole chemical business," she adds, referring to the body's release of endorphins and enkephalins into the bloodstream during times of extreme physical exertion—a physiological phenomenon that produces a mildly narcotic feeling—"happens to me in a very strong way, and I come out of class forgetting completely that I was depressed.

"I think dancing has been better than seeing a psychiatrist in keeping me healthy mentally."

Athletes frequently refer to the "high" induced by strenuous physical exertion. Dancing can help outdistance all of the mad, crazy, angry feelings that can be so destructive to a productive, satisfying life.

Even so, many dancers often work themselves beyond the "narcotic" effects of exercise. "I am constantly draining myself and burning energy, even mentally," says Fernando Bujones.

"I can go for a couple of weeks under the heavy pressure," Merrill Ashley tells me, "and then suddenly I will just collapse and will need a couple of days of just lots of sleep and getting away from it all before I can start over again. But that was when I was under heavy pressure. Now, since I haven't been dancing an excessive amount—you know, four or five times a week, enough rehearsal, not too much pressure—I feel fine. I seem now to be able to work myself up to the point of that good nervous tension that I need, and not feel wiped out afterward."

"Whatever you do, whether it's good or bad, there's no point in getting freaked about it," says Christopher D'Amboise, son of Jacques and a rising young star with the New York City Ballet, about the difficulty of coping with career stress. "But I still haven't learned that lesson yet. I go into each season optimistically, but halfway through I forget it.

"That's why I think that one of the healthiest things is to have a relationship with someone outside of the company . . . to have a girlfriend who is not in the company, because she can help you keep your perspective. Someone not in the company will say, 'What are you getting so upset about?'

Christopher D'Amboise of NYCB in *Gershwin Concerto* by Jerome
Robbins. *(Photo copyright by Steven Caras)*

"They have other interests and they can see when you're getting really crazy about some minor triviality, and make you realize how silly it is."

It is possible to overdo the best of things, including dance. That's why it is absolutely vital to be moderate and controlled in approaching this strenuous activity. During a wonderful career Suzanne Farrell has learned invaluable lessons about herself and about how to deal with stress.

"You have to learn to anticipate what you're doing, and to like what you're doing," Suzanne advises." I just became mentally relaxed and clear and open. And my health started to get better. It doesn't matter how well you take care of yourself, vitamin-wise or medicine-wise, nothing is going to do you any good if you are not in control of your feelings and your nerves. Which is very hard to do, and I guess not many people ever even get to that point.

"I try not to get angry . . . I don't fight, because I end up getting too upset, and I'm not able to knock that off too easily. So I don't fight with people I love, and I don't care to fight with people I don't care about.

"Having that kind of healthy attitude has helped me. Perhaps I've learned this by getting older, but I have begun to see that it can work well for everyone.

"I seem to be more involved in my work now than I ever thought I would be, which is very strange, because usually when you get to this point, you like to think of quitting. But I can't . . .

"Part of it is probably due to the fact that I did leave the company and go somewhere else," she says, referring to her five years with Maurice Béjart's Ballet of the Twentieth Century in Brussels, from 1970 to 1975. "I would live it all over again the same way, but while I was there I learned to relax. Somehow, in New York, you never learn to relax. I mean, I love New York, as far as dance and ballet go, and this is the *only* place at the present. But it means that all the bad things that go along with all the special, good things are much more traumatic than they would be somewhere else.

"So I learned how to relax. I don't know if it's so much to my credit, or if I was just put in a situation which wasn't as traumatic or as demanding as the one I had left. I really began to realize how important nerves are. I mean, you have to be nervous . . . nervous is good. It means anticipation.

"I feel that, over the years, when you do a ballet it should get easier. God is very wise in giving you enough time to learn how to cope, because you have to. Over the years, things should get easier.

"You know, I would certainly like to think that, my goodness, *Chaconne* shouldn't be as difficult now as it was before, because I've had the experience of doing it. Whether it's a good or bad performance, it happens—you can't always bat a thousand. But it shouldn't be as tiring as it used to be. Otherwise, what is the point of ever doing it again, if everything is going to be just as hard? Things should get easier. . . ."

On the Subject of Doctors

Sometimes dancers rely as heavily on a trusted doctor as they do on their trainer or masseur. A good doctor can help an injured dancer get back onstage sooner than he or she thought possible, or can help a dancer find relief from chronic aches and pains.

In a way, doctors are the dancers' mechanics, fine-tuning their bodies so they can perform at peak levels. Like everyone else, though, dancers often tend to forget about doctors until they are needed.

I was never susceptible to colds or flu, and somehow always believed it was due to being a healthy dancer. Then, when I was thirty-four, sailing along as everybody else caught flus and viruses, I suddenly found I had succumbed to the mumps. I was flabbergasted!

Frequently, however, dancers are frustrated by doctors who are not sensitive to their special needs. Because a dancer must rely on his or her body in making a living, a dancer's doctor must make allowances: allowing the dancer's body enough time to heal or strengthen, while taking into consideration that body's superior conditioning, for instance. The doctor must also try to prescribe treatments that won't debilitate a working dancer, especially in terms of broken bones or injured muscles and tendons.

Fernando Bujones describes his experiences with doctors during a recent injury. "When I had just recently injured my foot, I went to see several doctors. They took X rays and had different opinions about the different little pains I was feeling in my foot and ankle. One said I had a small bone spur and another one said something different. . . . I also went to a chiropractor, who said it was just tender, nothing more. Three or four different opinions . . .

"Finally, I went to the beach for three days, kept my foot in the water and got some sun. I said to myself, 'I am going to get better. I am going to do exercises in the water and start jumping on the foot to give it strength—to strengthen the ligaments I had slightly strained. I am not going to think about the diagnosis of a bone spur on the side. I am going to jog along the beach, and I'm going to do it. . . .'

"I did it with pain, but I did it. I danced five performances after just three weeks. I wasn't really all the way back, but I danced five performances without injuring it more. It's getting better every day, although it isn't there yet, but I am not going to see another doctor to tell me that it's better, but still a little bone spur.

"I'm not going to see him until one day when the foot starts crying for help again," Fernando continues. "Then I will think about what I should do. But that's the way I work—I don't look for trouble. I let trouble look for me, do you understand?

"You see doctors as you need them, but there is not one specific doctor who can help. I think that in the end, *we* are the ones who can help ourselves more than anyone else, not a doctor. I never believe in just one doctor's opinion. I try to mix them all together and make my own decision. I try to be the best person to help myself."

Merrill Ashley has a similar point of view. "I don't want to say that I never go to doctors. I do rely on them. But in a way, I feel that we all have to be our own doctors. I mean, I'm not against going to doctors and getting their advice—hearing what they have to say. I like to collect opinions and then decide myself. Because so frequently I feel that whatever they say to me has nothing to do with what I am feeling, or with what is really wrong with me. I feel I know much better.

"That whole thing with my hip, for example. If I had put myself in the hands of one doctor, God knows where I'd be today. I don't think I would be here in one piece. When they don't know what else to do it's 'Oh, let's operate. Just to see what happens.'

"I do understand doctors' frustration, but I would rather go searching for other opinions in other areas. Who knows where you're going to find an answer?"

Understandably, dancers are very cautious about placing the care of their bodies in the hands of doctors. Very often a dancer's entire future career depends upon the proper treatment of an injury. Most dancers stick with a doctor they feel is attuned to their particular requirements, in terms of health and in terms of their careers.

Cynthia Harvey had to search for the right doctor when she injured her hip a few years ago. "I think I found the right one when I went to the Manhattan Chiropractic Center. He was the first one on my list but the last one I went to, because I didn't know him. I had been to every other doctor. I went every-

NYCB's Merrill Ashley in *Ballo della Regina* by George Balanchine.
(Photo copyright © 1983 by Martha Swope)

where—I even went to faith healers in London. Nothing worked.

"No one could tell me what was wrong. I was beginning to think, Put yourself into an institution. So I finally went to this doctor, and he just poked and prodded. He also did a muscle test. He said, 'You know, it's not your hip that's the problem, it's your hamstrings.' He started giving me therapy, and it was like a miracle—in a month the pain was gone.

"I had been looking for help for six months, and I had been compensating for the pain. So that's when my foot went bad. He explained to me what I was doing by overcompensating. I was lucky to find him.

"Lucia [Chase, ABT's artistic director until her retirement in 1980, when Mikhail Baryshnikov assumed the role] was always very nice to me. 'Take as long as you need,' she'd always say. Misha says the same thing. He can also always suggest the best doctors to you: 'You should see so and so, or this or that therapist.'" Cynthia laughs. "It's good, because his recommendation will help you get better, and hopefully quicker, medical attention."

On the Subject of Smoking

No subject seems to divide dancers' opinions more widely than smoking. Dancers fall more or less into two camps on the subject: those who smoke and say it doesn't have a detrimental effect on their performance, and those who abhor the habit and would never dream of indulging in it. One thing is clear—dancers feel very strongly about the habit.

"To me it is crazy," says Fernando Bujones. "You lose your wind, you begin to cough, you cut your stamina in half. And dancing is already so difficult—you need to have all of your stamina and all of your energy. Especially male dancers. Perhaps a ballerina can get away with it, because her variations and her jumps are not as demanding as a male dancer's. For a male dancer to smoke like a chimney and expect to jump solo for two and a half minutes and still look strong, you know, it is very difficult.

"Smoking is something that, I have the feeling, you pay a price for sooner or later. You have to be very, very careful."

"I would tell dancers not to start smoking," agrees Heather Watts. "Don't start. Really, it's dirty. You know you *feel* dirty."

"I don't know how anybody can smoke," says Peter Fonseca. Merrill Ashley declares, "I am an avid nonsmoker," and Martine van Hamel adds, "Nobody should smoke."

Not only do some dancers maintain that they couldn't and wouldn't ever smoke, but many find the habit of others offensive. George Balanchine, a reformed smoker, detested it and wouldn't let anyone smoke around him. Christopher D'Amboise says, "I can't believe people smoke. I see people, and I won't mention names, but I see them out in the main hall warming up for a performance and they smell like dancers *after* a performance. Here I am leaving the barre, and there's someone else doing a barre and we both finish about the same time. When he finishes, he lights up a cigarette and I think, Here you are, about to be going out onto the stage and you are smoking. How on earth can you do that? I can't even breathe!"

Dierdre Carberry also complains about the annoyance of others' smoke. "I can't take it. Being around smokers for a long period, the smoke just gets to my head and I suffocate. I can't breathe when they smoke."

On the other hand, of course, there are a number of very fine dancers who do smoke and who don't seem to be adversely affected by it. Baryshnikov, Makarova and Goudenov are well-known smokers—so visible in fact that many people think it is a Russian habit. "It seems beyond my comprehension," says Fer-

Alexander Godunov of ABT. *(Photo copyright by W. Reilly)*

nando Bujones. "Many of [the Russian dancers] smoke and drink vodka. I can't understand how they can drink vodka so much—sometimes half a bottle after an evening performance. I wouldn't be able to get up the next morning if I did that."

Scientific studies all point to the fact that smoking has an adverse effect on your health, but if we take dancers as our example, it's obvious that some people are more able than others to cope with the loss of lung-power and stamina that smoking causes.

Of course, it's not true that only the Russian dancers are smokers, nor do any other general assumptions hold true. Like the rest of the general public, a percentage of dancers have become addicted to smoking regardless of health considerations.

While on the subject of addictive habits, a few words about dancers and the destructive influences of alcohol and drugs may be appropriate here.

Like the rest of the nation, dancers face the temptations of alcohol and drug abuse in today's social and career scenes. There are the misguided who begin by consuming drugs or alcohol, and end by having it consume them. Unlike the rest of society, however, dancers who are physically dependent upon drugs and alcohol are usually weeded out of the ballet world. If dancers performed only once a week it might be possible for someone to get away with such destructive habits—for a while. But in most major ballet companies, dancers are rehearsing and performing nearly every day during the season. And they just can't do drugs or get bombed regularly, because the aftereffects will prevent them from putting out the 110 percent that is required of a performer.

Dancers spend the best part of their lives pursuing their art. They deny themselves, they deprive themselves, they drive themselves, all in order to dance for a few years. To sabotage that pursuit is unthinkable . . . usually. To cut weeks or months or years out of a promising career is a terrible tragedy. Most dancers aren't willing to risk that.

On the Subject of Vitamins and Health

Despite the fact that maintaining an active life is inherently healthy, dancers almost always feel compelled to further that healthy edge with vitamin supplements (which also help to re- place any vitamin deficiency caused by a low-calorie diet).

Isabel Brown claims that she raised her children on multiple vitamins. She especially recommends the B vitamins and vita- min C, one for "nerves" and the other for "colds." Still, Isabel is convinced that it isn't vitamins, ". . . but just the physical ac- tivity that makes dancers healthier than most people."

Suzanne Farrell, on the other hand, doesn't feel the need for a vitamin supplement, stating flatly, "I don't take vitamins." Peter Fonseca agrees. "I just don't like to *have* to have vitamins or protein powder, or to have this, that or the other. Because when you have to have all of that, all of a sudden you're in a situation where, if you don't get it, you start to say, 'Now I don't have my stuff, and I'm never going to make it through the day,' or, 'I'm not going to make it through a performance.'"

On the other hand, Fernando Bujones feels certain that tak- ing vitamins has helped him deal with injuries, and he takes vitamins C and B-12 regularly, and sometimes E. "My fear, how- ever, is of giving the body too much of any one thing," he says. "I think that that's bad, just like if you smoke too much it's bad. If you drink too much it's bad, and if you take too many vitamins it's bad."

One subject on which almost all dancers agree is the detri- mental effects of junk food, overprocessed food and the like. Isabel says she never gave her children junk foods. "They got their share of that in school. We called them 'empty calories.' I avoid cookies and cakes, and even cereal, which I think is deadly for children unless it's the natural kind without sugar coatings."

While some dancers will eat only health food, others try not to become too fussy or gimmicky about their diets. Lots of health kicks have made the rounds of ballet companies over the years, but dancers still find that proper diet and proper rest are the best ways to stay healthy.

"I find that when I eat the least and work the hardest," said Peter Fonseca, "I get the least sick. I try to keep my meals balanced and get enough sleep, which are the only two things for staying healthy. And I find that when I'm working hard, I sleep the best."

For Martine van Hamel it's ". . . physical exercise. That alone keeps people fairly healthy. When you are functioning well mentally and physically, you tend to respond most naturally to what you take into your body."

"Health is the most important thing a person has," says Mel Tomlinson. "Not money, but health . . . Proper rest and nutrition mean having good health."

Yet Christopher D'Amboise warns that "a healthy attitude is more important than worrying about your health." Being over-protective about your health, or worrying too much about it, can impair your ability to function. Any dancer who cancels performances regularly out of obsessive fears for his or her health will soon notice other dancers getting the parts.

Basically, the dancers are advising you not to overdo it—not in dieting, not in exercising, not in vitamins, not in smoking, not in anything. Summing it up, Mel Tomlinson says, "Too much junk is bad, but so is too much health food!"

Martine Van Hamel of ABT in *Push Comes to Shove* by Twyla
Tharp. *(Photo copyright © 1983 by Martha Swope)*

CHAPTER ELEVEN
Seven Diet Sins

These seven diet sins are traps you must avoid if you are to benefit from the advice in the book—seven temptations that will torpedo the best-laid plans of any diet or exercise plan.

Sin Number One: Snacking

More diets are wrecked by snacking than by any other temptation. We're bombarded by advertisements of all sorts for snacks, salty or sweet, highly processed or all-natural, but all extremely high in "empty" calories.

Most Americans become addicted to snacking from an early age. Unfortunately for snack addicts, when it comes time to lose weight, the urge for just a little something between meals becomes virtually overpowering. Dancers are certainly not immune to the call of the wild chocolate bar—in fact, if there's no time for a proper lunch, many dancers will indulge in an on-the-run snack instead.

"My favorite snack is sugar," confesses Jean-Pierre Bonnefous. "It's the worst thing for me, but it's what I like." Patty McBride adds, "Sometimes I love a beautiful, sinful, 'sometimes' food!" "I snack on cookies," admits Mel Tomlinson. "I love to snack . . . but at least they're granola cookies."

If snacking is a sometimes indulgence, it's not necessarily de-

203 ·

structive to a diet. However, one good snack usually leads to another, and it isn't long before snacking calories add up.

Once you've given in to the snacking temptation, you'll discover what all sinners come to in the end: contrition. "I was with Jacques [D'Amboise]," said Isabel Brown, "who's trying to diet for the season. He had pecan pie with whipped cream at lunch, and four hours later moaned to me, 'Why did I have that pie?' Obviously, it had been on his mind for four hours! Dancers think about food all the time."

On the subject of snacks that seem low-calorie or dietetic but have as many calories as well-known fattening foods, Isabel says, "If you talk about a yogurt in a cone which has been flavored, then you're talking about something almost as bad as ice cream and it just ruins a diet. It still may be less fattening than ice cream, but not that much less fattening."

If the urge to snack is your undoing, the most successful way for you to combat that may be to make snacking a part of your diet. With the small but nutritious meals of the Dancers' Diet, one or even two snacks a day can fit into your calorie allotment without upsetting your diet at all. The important thing to remember is that you can't let yourself go when it comes to snacks—no finishing off the bag of potato chips, no nibbling on cookies, no midnight raid into the refrigerator or the cupboard.

"Good" snacks:

one cup of plain popcorn	40 calories
one medium apple	80 calories
one-half cantaloupe	66 calories
one small orange	65 calories
one medium peach	35 calories
one cup of diced pineapple	76 calories
ten large strawberries	37 calories
one medium tangerine	40 calories
one whole, large dill pickle	7 calories
one medium stalk of raw celery	5 calories

one whole raw carrot	20 calories
one average raw cucumber	31 calories
one medium green pepper	15 calories

Rules to follow when indulging your snack cravings:

- Have low-calorie snacks ready and waiting for times of temptation.

- Don't be spontaneous about snacking—either plan your snacks or go without them.

- Don't have high-calorie snacks in your home—if that means throwing away the unfinished half-gallon of ice cream, do it now!

Sin Number Two: Eating Junk Food

Dancers advise against junk food, not only when dieting but any time. When dancers look for foods that are high in energy without being high in calories, junk food never fits the bill.

It may be tempting to take advantage of convenience foods or fast foods when a busy schedule precludes taking the time for a decent meal. But one can almost always avoid junk foods. One popular fast-food restaurant in the Lincoln Center area sells lots of yogurt to ballet students and professionals. Yogurt, while relatively high in calories (about 250 in one cup), provides nutrition that is vastly superior to the 150 empty calories in a one-ounce bar of chocolate. If a balanced meal is not possible because of time or circumstance, it is still a good idea to avoid junk food altogether.

Baryshnikov heartily disapproves of junk food—whether in America or in Russia (which is how he characterizes the high-carbohydrate menu of the Soviet ballet school). "They fed us

NYCB's Roma Sosenko attending to her toes. *(Photo copyright by Steven Caras)*

mostly junk food—and we used to eat four meals a day. Now I eat quite a heavy breakfast, and if I am performing I eat after the performance, with a light lunch during the afternoon. You know, a little soup or a sandwich or something like that." With a hearty breakfast, Misha feels he can get through the day with just a light lunch. "I eat eggs and bacon for breakfast, and I prefer tea to coffee."

So how does he get through the demands of a long evening performance?

"Actually, I like a pot of tea with lemon and honey. That is very nice. I often drink that during intermission—I need it."

A dancer's schedule is probably the greatest hindrance to eating balanced meals at reasonable hours. But few dancers resort to junk foods to see them through a hectic day or when on tour.

Sin Number Three: Undereating and Bad Nutrition

Sin Number Three may be even worse than Numbers One and Two. For if snacking can ruin a diet and junk food is counterproductive, undereating and bad nutrition can ruin your health. If carried to extremes, it can kill you. While it may be true that you can never be too rich, in some cases you *can* be too thin.

To Cynthia Harvey, slenderness brings added grace and beauty to the dancer's line—the outline of the appearance on-stage—the relationship of arms, legs, head, hands and feet to the body. "But I don't want to see bones either," she warns. "I rarely get bony unless I get sick."

Because there is such a fine line between just right and too thin for ballerinas, they must always be careful to keep on the healthy side of that line. Natalia Makarova, who is very thin, seems to have set a standard for her fellow dancers, but other

American Ballet Theatre company members warn her to maintain a healthy minimum weight.

"Sometimes she runs the risk of getting too thin as a woman, although she looks very, very good for a ballerina," says Fernando Bujones. "People have told her, 'You know, you're getting too thin.' Once Marcia, my wife, and I told her she was so thin you could see the bones sticking out even more than ever. We pointed out to her that it can be dangerous to let yourself go to such an extreme without even realizing it. Some of the girls in our company have been injured because the nutrition of their diets is so bad. They've become careless and don't eat properly."

Many ballerinas have experimented with extreme diets, sacrificing nutrition for fast weight loss. "I decided I wasn't going to eat for a while," confesses Martine van Hamel. "I went to bed, not eating anything for a couple of days. When I tried to go back to work, it was a week before I could do anything, because I had gotten so weak from fasting."

One such experience is usually enough to make an aspiring dancer stick to nutritious methods of dieting. But often the side effects of a nutritional imbalance are not so easily discernible. I recall one student who suffered from severe headaches. When her doctor finally diagnosed them as the consequences of a protein deficiency, she complained, "But protein is so expensive!"

Heather Watts talked about the effects of low weight on her mental and emotional state. "When [the company] was in Russia, I had a strange experience. The food there made me so sick I almost didn't eat at all for five weeks. I really got quite ill, but being that thin makes your head feel light—a very weird feeling. That made me realize how anorexia, the eating disorder, is a very strange and serious problem."

While Heather's nutritional deficiencies resulted in illness, she was probably not suffering from anorexia nervosa. Her "fasting" came from an intolerance of the foreign food, and not from a compulsion to be thin.

There seems to be a common misconception about anorexia nervosa among the general public, and among dancers too, that it can be caused by an excessive weight-loss diet, that losing weight can somehow tip the balance for a young woman and turn her into an anorectic. The medical profession takes a different view, however.

"It is erroneous to equate anorexia nervosa with simply 'going overboard' on a diet," writes Dr. L. M. Vincent in his *Competing with the Sylph, Dancers and the Pursuit of the Ideal Body Form* (Fairway, KS.: Andrews and McMeel, 1979). The underlying causes of anorexia nervosa are related to personality and environmental factors, and are not the result of nutritional deficiencies or fasting. Unnatural thinness is the symptom of the disorder, and not the cause.

This severe, debilitating and sometimes life-threatening disorder does occur among dancers and, of course, does enormous harm to otherwise promising careers. Dancers, teachers, coaches and management must all be aware of the symptoms of the illness, as well as its serious consequences, although spotting an anorectic among a corps of thinner-than-normal dancers would be difficult for anyone but a trained observer. The signs of personality disturbances are a more accurate gauge than is a sudden or drastic weight loss. If there is *any* question about this disorder, however, see the doctor at once.

This may be the place to remind you of the second rule of the Dancers' Diet: Eat a well-rounded, balanced variety of foods. This is a special warning to those dieters who are prepared to starve themselves in order to reach a dangerously low weight: If your weight falls even five pounds below the recommended weight range for your height in the table on page 32, *contact your doctor.* No one should maintain such a low weight without medical supervision.

And as a further warning for aspiring dancers: Please don't think that being unnaturally thin is expected of you, or even that it will give you a competitive edge. Success in ballet will only come through strength, artistry and ability. You must be thin, but the most important message of this book is not to overdo it.

Be moderate, reasonable and *use your common sense.*

Sin Number Four: Not Getting Enough Rest

Mikhail Baryshnikov says he needs a full night's sleep. "A minimum of eight hours. That's the *minimum.* Actually, between nine and ten would be best. When I go to sleep at about eleven o'clock, let's say, I wake up about nine or ten hours later."

For dancers, who are strenuously active several hours a day nearly every day, sleep isn't a luxury, it's a necessity.

Mel Tomlinson says, "We don't seem to get enough rest during our day. The day is occupied with classes and rehearsals, and rest helps to restore us, give us new life and a new beginning."

Heather Watts complains that after the excitement of a performance, she often has trouble sleeping. "I stay up very late after a performance. I'm too excited to actually go to bed. I am usually not able to nap, so I'm selective about sleeping. I always have needed a great deal of sleep and until recently always felt robbed if I didn't get ten or twelve hours of it. Of course, I never could, but if I go to bed at three o'clock, realizing that I have to get up at nine, I'll be depressed about it. So I try to sleep later in the mornings. I always try to steal an extra snooze."

Mel Tomlinson also finds it difficult to relax and fall asleep after a performance. "If I'm rehearsing, I can sleep well. If I'm performing, though, I have trouble because my thoughts are geared toward the next day, and I find myself restless and dancing in my sleep. In order to unwind, I take a hot bath. That relaxes me and then I start to fall asleep early in the evening."

"I can sleep seven or eight hours," claims Edward Villella.

"But on an airplane, I'm only able to fall asleep for a half-hour or so. So I'll have to catch up—like during my massage, I'll fall asleep."

"I don't function well if I don't get enough sleep," agrees Merrill Ashley. "If I don't sleep well, I can't do anything well."

Patricia McBride and Jean-Pierre Bonnefous rely on sleep to restore energy. "I've always been lucky," says Patricia. "You know, I've always been a sleeper. When I'm tired, if I can get enough sleep, then I don't really hurt. I can wake up and feel really rested the next morning, even after a horrendous day. I've never had a problem with energy because it's really easy for me to sleep.

"Now that our baby's arrived, my whole sleeping cycle has changed. I sleep two or three hours maybe, and I feel great. It's so strange, but I don't need a lot of sleep now.

"Jean-Pierre is different though," she laughs.

"Sometimes I get up in the middle of the night," Jean-Pierre adds, "and I get so mad at Patty, because she is getting such a good rest and I can't sleep.

"Usually in tense situations, it's hard for me to sleep, but the more tense a situation becomes, the calmer Patty becomes."

While dancers recommend getting enough sleep for health and fitness—a full night's sleep is vital—without relaxation, the full benefits of sleep are lacking.

A tense or stressful lifestyle brings on both mental and physical exhaustion, regardless of the amount of sleep you're getting. Dance, like any other highly competitive profession, brings out a compulsive drive that can consume dancers. Cynthia Harvey describes the experience of first facing that pressure.

"My first nine months in [American Ballet Theatre] I worked like a crazy person. I had been in the scholarship class before joining, and I used to watch the company from up above and think, How can they sit on the floor during their breaks? They should be working!

"I decided then," she continues, "that when I got into the

"I've realized that you learn to take a rest," says Cynthia Harvey.
(Photo copyright © 1983 by James J. Camner)

company, I was going to work really hard. Well, I did, and I didn't sit once and I never took a lunch break. I went to every-one else's rehearsal as well as my own, and I worked very, very hard. After the big ABT tour, everyone took a vacation, but I worked harder. I took three classes a day, because, you know, you don't get any better unless you work. I was just so happy to be in the company.

"It got so bad, though, that even when Rudolf [Nureyev] would come in and start doing warm-ups, I'd just fall asleep in the middle of the floor. I was really ready for a vacation.

"Since then, I've realized that you learn to take a rest."

Most dancers, as they grow older and wiser, learn that you can accomplish as much, if not more, by getting the proper sleep and sufficient rest than you can if you work yourself to the point of collapse. You will find yourself becoming more productive and your performance improving, whether you're onstage or at a desk.

Sin Number Five: Inactivity

Sin Number Five is the opposite extreme of Sin Number Four. If not getting enough rest is bad for you, so is the sin of inactivity. Dancers are unanimous in claiming good health as one of the benefits of an active life.

Leading such active lives, dancers find inactivity intolerable, and associate it with dullness, tiredness, headaches, nervous-ness, etc.

Beyond questions of health, however, dancers also point to the mental benefits of activity: "A zest for life," "You feel more alive," "It helps you sleep," "You enjoy life more."

"Laying off because of an injury," says Fernando Bujones, "is a little frustrating because I don't like to sit for a long time in one place just waiting for something to heal. It drives me up a wall. I want to do something. I want to start exercising and moving around."

If you benefit from this book in any way, it should be from dancers' advice to keep active. Madame Danilova has followed this advice her entire life. "One must take very good care of oneself. If you think you are getting old perhaps, you just get upset. But if you keep busy . . . I mean, everybody will just grow old with you. Everybody is like the flowers—you know, change the water and when we are ready, we just close ourselves up. But I think, in the meantime, keep very busy."

In one way, the sin of inactivity is the greatest sin because it means you are ignoring many of life's potentials, and you are letting your body go to waste.

Sin Number Six: Not Knowing Your Own Limits

It is important to remember, when you are preparing for a weight-loss diet or a physical-fitness regimen, that everyone has a set of limitations for his or her own body.

You can only take your body so far. You can exercise it, hone it, work it, reduce it as much as you possibly can. While you'll end up healthy and trim, you probably won't ever be a Baryshnikov.

"A lot of it has to do with the basic body build," says Marika Molnar. "Anatomically, some people are just born with a better bone structure than others, or the muscles are distributed around the bones with a better leverage system to pull the bones with."

In other words, you can start with two dancers of the same height and weight and give them both exactly the same training, and yet one will manage to become stronger, or more supple, or have greater stamina than the other in the end. How do dancers work with their limitations?

"It is really very important to know your own body type. For instance, certain dancers should really get in to class half an hour early in order to warm up properly. Because of their body types, it takes them longer," Marika advises.

"I would expect the people with longer legs and arms to be more successful in ballet than the people who have longer torsos and shorter legs and arms. Of course, ideally, we all look for a well-proportioned body."

This is not to say that there is a pattern piece ballet dancers must conform to, however. There are any number of examples of very great dancers whose ability or artistry overcame physical disadvantages. While body type is a significant factor in determining a dancer's success or failure, there are no hard and fast rules to follow.

But an individual's limitations are important in knowing what is and what is not possible to accomplish. Setting reasonable goals, whether they are easy or difficult to achieve, is possible only when you know your own body, its capabilities and its limitations. By all means, set high standards and dream impossible dreams, but first, be honest with yourself.

The price you pay for being unaware of the limit of your body's capabilities is pain and, even worse, lasting injury.

"I think dancers really don't know how to judge pain and injury," observes Merrill Ashley. "They are never told how to take care of those things. Only since Marika Molnar joined the company has there been any attempt to teach us when to use ice or heat on an injury, or how to stretch before a performance."

One decision all dancers must face sooner or later in their careers is how soon to return to work after an injury. Over the course of many years they learn from experience when the time comes for dancing and when it's time to hold back. Merrill suffered an injury recently and has gained some painful insight into that very question.

"You have to experience it yourself. Dancers won't listen to advice, whether to rest or take time off, and no one can make them. It's only when you've been out for a long time that you learn how to come back from a bad injury, which can be a difficult thing to do.

"People will tell you to come back slowly, but dancers don't know what 'slowly' means. To them, maybe it's a week. You know, the first day you do barre work, the second day you do a little more, and the third day you are up to jumps and a little point work. By the end of the week, you are doing big jumps. And that's slowly to most dancers.

"A week coming back after six weeks off? And then the dancers want to know why they're hurting. I think the school should hold a short clinic: a week of practice to show you the basic way to take care of yourself."

Without question, dancers feel great pressure to return to work after injury. The company is depending on you; your career seems to depend on it; your friends tell you you can do it. Once again, though, you're asking for trouble unless you know your limits.

In conditioning yourself, whether it's after an injury or just to improve in specific areas, it's vital that you work closely with a doctor and a therapist. Don't overdo it. Be careful and follow their professional advice.

This is as true for non-dancers as it is for dancers. In diet and in physical fitness, push your body; challenge it, of course. But don't drive your body when it tells you through pain, discomfort, dizziness, shortness of breath or any other signs, that you have arrived at its limit.

It is possible to increase the body's endurance systematically. That's why the levels of physical activity listed in Chapter Nine recommend a gradual increase of activity. However, you will not improve your fitness if you regularly punish your body with over-strenuous or otherwise inappropriate exercise or diet.

It all boils down once again to moderation, patience and knowing your own body.

Sin Number Seven: Neglecting Your Equipment

"Misha, what is the single most important thing a young dancer should do?"

"The single most important thing," he answers, ". . . wash your tights!"

From the oldest pair of tights to the newest pair of toe shoes, dancers take care of their equipment because training and performance can depend on it. But the most essential piece of equipment, the body, needs even more care.

That, basically, is what this book is about: diet, health and fitness. How to take care of the world's greatest machine.

What the dancers have said in so many different ways is, if you treat your body right—giving it the proper nourishment and sufficient exercise, conditioning it and keeping it healthy—your reward will be something that many would give millions for, but which is priceless: the unmistakable feeling of well-being, physical and mental.

Mikhail Baryshnikov. (*Photo copyright by W. Reilly*)

APPENDIX:
The Reading List

Through *The Dancers' Body Book*, we've looked at the importance of proper diet, nutrition, conditioning and exercise, not only to professional dancers but to the general public as well.

For those of you who would now like to explore the world of dance even further, here is a list of books, guides and articles that deal with some of the specific subjects of diet, health and exercise from a dancer's viewpoint. Also included are two excellent pamphlets that can readily be obtained from the U. S. Government Printing Office.

Arnheim, Daniel D. *Dance Injuries, Their Prevention and Care.* St. Louis: Mosby, 1980.

Friedman, Philip, and Eisen, Gail. *The Pilates Method of Physical and Mental Conditioning.* New York: Warner, 1981.

Grant, Gail. *Technical Manual and Dictionary of Classical Ballet.* New York: Dover, revised republication, 1967.

Jacob, Ellen, and Jonas, Christopher. *Dance in New York, An Indispensable Companion to the Dance Capital of the World.* New York: Quick-Fox, 1980.

Kent, Allegra. *Allegra Kent's Water Beauty Book.* New York: St. Martin's Press, 1976.

Kirstein, Lincoln, Stuart, Muriel, and Dyer, Carlus. *The Clas-*

sic *Ballet, Basic Technique and Terminology,* with preface by George Balanchine. New York: Knopf, 1952.

McDonagh, Don. *How to Enjoy Ballet.* New York: Doubleday, 1978.

Micheli, Lyle J., M.D., Walasezk, Arleen, R.P.T., and Gerbino, Peter, M.A. "Are Ballerinas Physically Fit?" *Dancemagazine,* December 1981, p. 74.

Neale, Wendy. *Ballet Life Behind the Scenes.* New York: Crown, 1982.

―――. *On Your Toes, Beginning Ballet: A Complete Guide to Proper Ballet Training for Pre-kindergarten to Adult Beginners.* New York: Crown, 1980.

Newman, Barbara. *Striking a Balance, Dancers Talk About Dancing.* Boston: Houghton Mifflin, 1982.

Page, Louise, and Raper, Nancy. *Calories & Weight, The USDA Pocket Guide.* Washington, D.C.: Consumer Nutrition Center, Science and Education Administration, revised May 1981. Agriculture Information Bulletin Number 364.

―――. *Food and Your Weight.* Washington, D.C.: Consumer and Food Economics Institute, Agricultural Research Service, revised November 1977. U.S. Department of Agriculture, Home and Garden Bulletin No. 74.

Vincent, L. M., M.D. *Competing with the Sylph, Dancers and the Pursuit of the Ideal Body Form,* Fairway, Kan.: Andrews and McMeel, 1979.

―――. *The Dancer's Book of Health.* Fairway, Kan.: Andrews and McMeel, 1978.

4 3 4 2